Storytelling for Social Justice

Through accessible language and candid discussions, *Storytelling for Social Justice* explores the stories we tell ourselves and each other about race and racism in our society. Making sense of the racial constructions expressed through the language and images we encounter every day, this book provides strategies for developing a more critical understanding of how racism operates culturally and institutionally in our society. Using the arts in general, and storytelling in particular, the book examines ways to teach and learn about race by creating counter-storytelling communities that can promote more critical and thoughtful dialogue about racism and the remedies necessary to dismantle it in our institutions and interactions. Illustrated throughout with examples drawn from high school classrooms, teacher education programs, and K-12 professional development programs, the book provides tools for examining racism as well as other issues of social justice. For every teacher who has struggled with how to get the "race discussion" going or who has suffered through silences and antagonism, the innovative model presented in this book offers a practical and critical framework for thinking about and acting on stories about racism and other forms of injustice.

Lee Anne Bell is Professor and Barbara Silver Horowitz Director of Education at Barnard College, Columbia University.

The Teaching/Learning Social Justice Series

Edited by Lee Anne Bell, Barnard College, Columbia University

Storytelling for Social Justice

*Connecting Narrative and
the Arts in Antiracist Teaching*

Lee Anne Bell

 Routledge
Taylor & Francis Group

NEW YORK AND LONDON

KH

First published 2010
by Routledge
270 Madison Avenue, New York, NY 10016

Simultaneously published in the UK
by Routledge
2 Park Square, Milton Park, Abingdon, Oxon OX14 4RN

Routledge is an imprint of the Taylor & Francis Group, an informa business

© 2010 Taylor & Francis

Typeset in Caslon by EvS Communication Networx, Inc.
Printed and bound in the United States of America on acid-free paper by Walsworth
Publishing Company, Marceline, MO

Library of Congress Cataloging in Publication Data
A catalog record has been requested for this book

ISBN 10: (hbk) 0-415-80327-6
ISBN 10: (pbk) 0-415-80328-4
ISBN 10: (ebk) 0-203-85223-0

ISBN 13: (hbk) 978-0-415-80327-4
ISBN 13: (pbk) 978-0-415-80328-1
ISBN 13: (ebk) 978-0-203-85223-1

6/27/11

I dedicate this book to the emerging teachers in my classes at Barnard, to the young people in the New York City public schools where they learn to teach, and to the children and young adults in my personal life who fill me with delight and help me to stay hopeful about the future: my special sweeties Seth and Sumita, and Caridad Raven, Amara, Jessica, Emily, Fiona, Annie, John, Anthony, James and Joey. May your emerging/transforming stories keep us moving toward the better world you and your generation so deserve.

Contents

Acknowledgments

This book was enriched by the ideas, energy and creativity of so many people in my personal and professional life. The Storytelling Project Model at the heart of the project described here took shape during 2004–2005 through the collaborative work of an amazing creative team of artists, public school teachers, scholars and Barnard/Columbia undergraduates: Rosemarie Roberts, Roger Bonair-Agard, Thea Abu El-Haj, Dipti Desai, Kayhan Irani, Uraline Septembre Hager, Christina Glover, Anthony Asaro, Patricia Wagner, Zoe Duskin, Vicki Cuellar and Leticia Dobzinski. Our work together has been one of the high points of my professional life. I especially want to honor the contributions of Rosemarie Roberts who co-led the Storytelling Project with me as a post-doctoral fellow at Barnard from 2004 to 2007. Her insight, passion, commitment and wisdom were a constant source of inspiration throughout the three years we worked together.

Four Barnard/Columbia undergraduates worked with us in 2005–2006 to conduct research on the Storytelling Project Curriculum in two high school classrooms: Svati Lelyveld, Brett Murphy, Vanessa D'Egidio and Ebonie Smith. Their enthusiasm for the project and commitment to the high school youth with whom we worked were invaluable. I am grateful to the students, teachers and administrators in the small high school where we conducted our research for their responsiveness to this experiment and for the many insights they shared as we worked through the curriculum together.

This project would not have been possible without Marco Stoeffel and the Third Millennium Foundation who provided financial support and encouraged us to experiment and take risks. The International Center for Tolerance Education offered a spacious and inviting setting for our work as a creative team and for the summer institute for teachers where we first tested out the model.

A Visiting Research position at Vassar College in 2008 enabled me to work in a majestic library surrounded by beautiful grounds to walk when I needed a break from the world in my head. I am especially grateful to Chris Bjork and Chris Roellke who welcomed me to Vassar and provided friendship and support during my time there.

I could not have completed this book without the patience and support of my wonderful Barnard colleagues and a sabbatical that afforded essential time to immerse myself in the project and complete the manuscript. In particular, Maria Rivera and Lisa Edstrom have been unwavering in their support and I feel blessed to work with them on a daily basis.

At various times I was sustained by conversation with friends and colleagues who provided encouragement and a sounding board for my ideas: Maurianne Adams, Dipti Desai, Markie Hancock, Kayhan Irani, Jackie Irvine, Linda Marchesani, Ina Mitchell, Celia Oyler, Kathy Phillips and Ximena Zuniga. Kathy Phillips, in particular, read every word and offered insights and perspective from her decades of work as an educator and community activist. The book is immeasurably enriched by her close reading and detailed feedback.

Catherine Bernard, my superb editor at Routledge, was responsive and supportive throughout the project even as her second child and the completion of this book arrived at the same time!

I am indebted to the three anonymous readers who provided thoughtful, critical feedback on earlier drafts. Their comments pushed my thinking further and helped me keep my audience clearly before me as I wrote and revised.

I am lucky to participate in an embracing community of friends who are always available for encouragement, laughter, and welcome diversions. They are too many to name but please know that I love you all. Also, thank you Ami for helping me to learn to stay in the present moment and Anna for helping me to believe in my own voice.

Finally, I am so deeply grateful to Ravi who read draft after draft, cooked nourishing meals, dragged me out for walks and generally propped me up whenever my confidence and energy flagged. Your support and love make everything possible. I promise normal life can now resume!

INTRODUCTION

STORYTELLING AND THE SEARCH FOR RACIAL JUSTICE

Race Talk Matters

In the white community, the path to a more perfect union means acknowledging that what ails the African-American community does not just exist in the minds of black people; the legacy of discrimination—and current incidents of discrimination, while less overt than in the past—are real and must be addressed. Not just with words, but with deeds—by investing in our schools and our communities; by enforcing our civil rights laws and ensuring fairness in our criminal justice system; by providing this generation with ladders of opportunity that were unavailable for previous generations. It requires all Americans to realize that your dreams do not have to come at the expense of my dreams; that investing in the health, welfare, and education of black and brown and white children will ultimately help all of America prosper... Let us find that common stake we all have in one another, and let our politics reflect that spirit as well.

(Senator Barack Obama, Speech at Constitution Center, Philadelphia, March 18, 2008)

Senator and presidential candidate Barack Obama's speech on race at Constitution Center in Philadelphia on March 18, 2008 was in many ways historic. Former Kennedy speechwriter Ted Sorensen said, "I don't know of any presidential campaign speech by anyone, including even John F. Kennedy, that had as much courage and principle and long-term importance on the most fundamental problem that has faced this country since its founding, and that's the problem of race" (Paulson & Marks, 2008). Most rare for a politician, Senator Obama dared to talk openly and honestly about the history of racism in the

United States and how this legacy courses through the lives of people in all racial groups, shaping our institutions, experiences, consciousness and actions still today. He unsettled the typical narratives about race relations that circulate in mainstream media and popular culture, narratives that gloss over or oversimplify the realities of racism, invoking what Patricia Williams calls "premature community" (Williams, 1998), and, in so doing, block the awareness, knowledge and concerted action so necessary to finally progress on this matter.

Drawing attention to the legacy of slavery and legalized segregation and the legitimate frustration and anger within communities of color about the slow pace of change, Obama exposed a discourse that took by surprise white people who have few contacts where they might be privy to such sentiments. Pointing out the ways in which well-meaning white people, like his grandmother, unconsciously act on racial prejudice and stereotypes, he exposed the unacknowledged biases that haunt our interactions. Recognizing the resistance and confusion many white people express about a legacy to which they do not feel connected or responsible, Obama invited a larger, more sophisticated conversation than we have yet had on this topic, one that recognizes racial positions grounded in history with which we must finally contend as a nation if we are to live up to the democratic promises of our founding documents, to the American Dream.

I focus on the Obama speech not to talk about him as a person or public figure, but rather because as a contemporary public event witnessed and shared by a broad swath of our population, his speech offers a focal point for a discussion on race and racism. Following the speech, I was curious about how others responded to it and for weeks followed blogs, editorials and letters to editors. Many letters and comments attested to the hunger shared by many, from all racial groups, to have an honest discussion about how to address racism in this country. However, a great many were also from white writers angry that Obama raised these issues, incensed that he would imply that his grandmother was racist, and complaining that he was bringing in race where it didn't belong.

Mainstream commentators now use the election of our first black president as proof that our society has moved "beyond race" and that we are now a "post-racial" society. This inability or unwillingness to examine racial patterns and practices make it next to impossible to address racial discrimination and the very real barriers to access and opportunity that persist.

In July 2009 African American Harvard professor Henry Louis Gates, Jr. was arrested at his own home in broad daylight for "disorderly conduct" because he angrily demanded identification of the police officer standing in his kitchen. Gates had already shown proof that he lived there. The officer at that point knew the burglary call from a neighbor was mistaken, yet handcuffed Gates, put him into a police car, took him to the station and booked him. President Obama, when asked to comment on the incident by a reporter at a press conference, said he thought the police response was "probably stupid" later elaborating that it didn't make sense that it escalated to an arrest. The media discourse that followed this incident focused almost entirely around the issue of whether or not the case was about racial profiling by the police or playing the race card by Professor Gates. Very few commentators looked behind this incident in ways that could have broadened the discussion to examine historical and contemporary patterns and practices that impact the lives of large numbers of African Americans and other people of color consequentially on a daily basis. A myopic focus on the individual, idiosyncratic, and unique precluded a critical view of racial dynamics across time and space that would explain more accurately events in context.

While mainstream media downplay the role of race, right wing media discuss it incessantly, accusing President Obama of being racist in his comments on the Gates case and even of plotting a redistribution of wealth from Whites to people of color in a secret reparations scheme hidden within his health care reform proposals—turning reality completely on its head. The inability to discuss racism thoughtfully and critically in mainstream institutions makes it difficult to respond to overt racist talk from the right and, even more disturbing, to take steps to remedy the very real inequalities that persist. The disparities in assets and income between Whites and people of color, a legacy of slavery, Jim Crow and exclusionary land and social policies, have broadened in the 2009 recession, pushing many families of color past recession and into depression (Erenreich & Muhammad, 2009). An editorial in *The New York Times* notes that:

According to a 2008 report by United for a Fair Economy, a research and advocacy group, from 1998 to 2006 (before the sub-prime crisis), blacks lost $71 billion to $93 billion in home-value wealth from sub-prime loans. The researchers call this family net-worth catastrophe the "greatest loss of wealth in recent history for people of color." And the worst was yet to come. (Erenreich & Muhammad, 2009, p. 17)

The article goes on to provide examples of further losses for Blacks and other disenfranchised groups as the mortgage crisis ballooned. Yet, little commentary has explored the differential racial impacts of the bank bailout, the mortgage crisis, health care debates and other pressing problems. In the breach between rhetoric and reality, right wing media repeat the incredible claim that this president is secretly giving Blacks and other people of color a better deal at the expense of Whites.

How we talk about race matters. It provides a roadmap for tracing how people make sense of social reality, helping us to see where we connect with and where we differ from others in our reading of the world, and it defines the remedies that will be considered as appropriate and necessary. While talk in and of itself can't dismantle racism, a critical analysis of *how* we talk about racism as a society and as members of differently positioned racial groups, provides a way for us see ourselves and others more clearly, understand the racial system we have inherited, recognize the different roles played by Blacks, Whites and other racial groups in this history, and come to grips with the urgent work still to be done to dismantle racism and live up to the promises of equality in our national rhetoric and governing documents.

Storytelling for Social Justice focuses on race talk and the stories we tell ourselves and each other about race and racism in our society. The book presents a conceptual and pedagogical model for teaching about racism through examining the kinds of stories we tell and for imagining alternative stories that account for history, power and systemic, normalizing patterns to justify inequality. The Storytelling Project Model analyzes racism through four story types: stock stories, concealed stories, resistance stories and emerging/transforming stories. Using the arts in general, and storytelling in particular, the book examines ways to teach and learn about race by creating critical counter-storytelling communities that can promote more critical and thoughtful dialogue about racism and the remedies necessary to dismantle it in our institutions and interactions.

Chapter 1, "Critical Teaching about Racism through Story and the Arts," describes the Storytelling Project and introduces the theoretical framework for the Storytelling Project Model as a scaffold for organizing curriculum, teaching and training in different arenas. I review the four story types through which we conceptualize racial discourse in the model (stock stories, concealed stories, resistance stories and emerging/transforming stories) and discuss the challenges of creating community in which honest investigation of racial storytelling among diverse groups can take place. I discuss the power of the arts as a vehicle for examining racial stories in diverse communities and for helping us to imagine otherwise.

Chapter 2, "Stock Stories: Reproducing Racism and White Advantage," offers the first iteration of the Storytelling Project Model in practice, highlighting the construct of *stock stories*. I provide a definition of stock stories and discuss how they function to protect and reinforce the racial status quo. I use the example of the American Dream to illustrate how stock stories function and describe activities we developed in the project to deconstruct and critically analyze this iconic stock story.

Chapter 3, "Concealed Stories: Reclaiming Subjugated Memory and Knowledge," offers a second iteration of the Storytelling Project Model in practice, highlighting the story type of *concealed stories*. I define concealed stories and trace how they circulate within communities of color and among white racial progressives as sources of critical literacy and sustenance for survival in a racist society. I look at the role of social memory in perpetuating stock stories and the potential of memory work to expose and critique the self-interested nature of stock stories that are taken for granted as natural. I illustrate concealed stories through a visualization and writing activity that draws on racial memory to expose the genealogy of racism, tracing how individual stories are linked to broader patterns. I illustrate how we use juxtaposition of stock and concealed stories through visual art, versions of historical events and social science data and provide examples from the Storytelling Project Curriculum to illustrate our work with high school students.

Chapter 4, "Resistance Stories: Drawing on Antiracism Legacies and Contemporary Examples to Map the Future," turns to the third story type: *resistance stories*. This chapter offers a third iteration of the Storytelling Project Model in practice. I define resistance stories and discuss youth resistance as a valuable source for developing curriculum that engages concerns of young people to make education meaningful. Drawing on our research in two high school classrooms in New York City where the Storytelling Project Curriculum was enacted, I illustrate how we use resistance stories to look at racism through theater games, poetry, murals, oral history and action research in local communities.

Chapter 5, "Emerging/Transforming Stories: Challenging Racism in Everyday Life," offers a fourth iteration of the Storytelling Project Model in practice, highlighting the final story type of *emerging/transforming stories*. I define this story type and discuss why public schools, despite all their limitations, still offer an important site for struggle against racism and other forms of injustice. I use the example of an undergraduate teacher education seminar to demonstrate how the Storytelling Project Model can be used to help teachers understand racial positionality, think more critically about their practice, and develop curriculum that engages students as social critics and actors.

In Chapter 6, "Cultivating a Counter-Storytelling Community: The Storytelling Model in Action," I trace the Storytelling Model through a five-day intensive summer institute for teachers to illustrate the development of counter-storytelling community. I draw on theories of small group dynamics and intergroup dialogue to highlight stages in the development of critical storytelling community and to illustrate key points in the process.

My hope is that through becoming more aware of our racial narratives, their roots in our history and their role in sustaining institutional patterns of inequality that persist, we can be more receptive to the evidence of racial injustice around us, more thoughtful about remedies required and more urgent in our commitment to work for justice. While I focus in this book on racism, the four story types and the storytelling process can be used to critically examine other issues of social justice discussed in Adams, Bell and Griffin (2007). I have used the model to examine issues of sexism and anti-immigration policy, for example. *Storytelling for Social Justice* offers a practical, critical framework for thinking about and acting on stories about racism and other forms of injustice, historical and contemporary, to develop common ground with others to work for racial and social justice.

1

CRITICAL TEACHING ABOUT RACISM THROUGH STORY AND THE ARTS

Introducing the Storytelling Project Model[1]

> When we begin to see ourselves as contributing to a fabric, we are no longer invisible threads or entire bolts full of lonely self-importance.
>
> **(White student, 1995)**

The quote above comes from a paper written for a course in qualitative research where for two semesters we conducted interviews about race and racism in the United States with people working in education and human services (see L.A. Bell, 2003a). As we analyzed the transcripts of these interviews, I noticed how often people draw on stories to explicate their views about race, and the persistent ways that certain stories repeat, uttered as individual but patterned across multiple interviews. I also noticed that students who were more knowledgeable and conscious about racism (more often, though not exclusively, students of color), were able to comment on the racial assumptions embedded in stories in ways that enabled less aware classmates to discern racism through the vehicle of the words spread before them. When white students recognized themselves in these stories, for example, they were more open to reflecting on their own racial socialization in critical ways. It also seemed that students of color could point out the racist content of interviews without feeling they had to temper their insights to avoid defensiveness from white classmates. In one such discussion, a young white man commented in fascinated, dawning awareness, *"I've* said that before!" as he began to recognize and consider racial assumptions pointed out in the transcript he and an African American classmate were analyzing.

The focus on the words and stories of others prompted some of the least defensive, most honest and genuine conversations about racism I have witnessed in my teaching life.

I have been learning and teaching about racism for the past thirty years, experimenting with pedagogical approaches to racism and other forms of oppression, and exploring how to use as teaching tools the understanding I have gained about my own socialization and ongoing recruitment into whiteness. I have facilitated numerous courses and workshops on this topic in both all-white and mixed race groups and have witnessed the confusion, guilt, anger and resistance that many white students express at the idea that they have been socialized into a racialized system, as well as the anger, frustration and disillusionment shown by students of color who doubt that their own stories and experiences will ever be fully heard and understood. Though many times I see students come together as allies committed to work against racism, I feel dismay at the continual challenges of helping students hang onto an awareness of the systemic nature of racism in their lives and in the broader society.

How does studying the stories and words of others sometimes open up less defensive, more honest dialogue about racism and help students move to awareness of the systemic nature of white supremacy so much more quickly? How does this approach enable some white students to recognize their complicity in the racial system, and the damage of normative whiteness to themselves as human beings, as exemplified by the student I quoted at the opening of this chapter? These questions were the seeds for the Storytelling Project described in this book.

In this chapter, I introduce the Storytelling Project and the development of a pedagogical model for teaching about race and racism through storytelling and the arts. I trace the process through which the model was created, introduce four story types we use as constructs to explore race and racism, and discuss the central role of the arts in the model's development and implementation. This discussion lays the foundation for subsequent chapters that define in more detail each story type and describe pedagogical tools and activities we developed for using that story type to explore race and racism.

Creating the Storytelling Model

Kurt Lewin once said that there is nothing so practical as a good theory (Lewin, 1952). Our goals for the Storytelling Project were to experiment with the arts, and story in particular, to teach/learn about race and racism, and to develop practical pedagogical tools for teaching about racism that could be extended to other areas of social justice, replicated and adapted for a range of purposes and groups. We focused on strategies for curricular and professional development that would engage people both in critical examination of racism and in finding proactive ways to work against racism in their own communities. The Storytelling Model that emerged from this process views race and racism through four story types, drawing on multiple artistic and pedagogical tools to discover, develop and analyze stories about racism that can catalyze consciousness and commitment to action.

Our creative team of artists, educators, academics and undergraduate students met monthly for intensive full-day exploration and discussion of racism through various art forms. This incredibly generative process was facilitated by a grant from the Third Millennium Foundation and space for our work at their International Center for Tolerance Education (ICTE). Housed in a renovated warehouse in the DUMBO area of Brooklyn, ICTE provided a bright and open space, filled with art and surrounded by an expanse of river and sky visible from every window. Once a month we converged on this space to engage pedagogical and artistic processes for exploring racism.

Our starting point was a social justice education paradigm that looks at diversity through the structural dynamics of power and privilege. We were concerned with both diversity—how race is constructed as a form of difference—and social justice—the unequal ways in which social hierarchies sort difference to the benefit of some groups over others (Adams, Bell & Griffin, 2007). Using this focus we explored how racial stories and storytelling both reproduce and challenge the racial status quo and how methods derived from storytelling and the arts might help us expose and constructively analyze pervasive patterns that perpetuate racism in daily life. We examined the power *in* stories and the power dynamics *around* stories to help us understand how social location (our racial position in society) affects storytelling and to consider ways to generate new stories that account for power, privilege and position in discussing and acting on racial and other social justice issues. In particular, we wanted to expose and confront color-blind racism and develop tools to tackle racial issues consciously and proactively in a racially diverse group.

In our collective reading we examined theoretical ideas about race (identity, positionality, racial formations) and racism (power, privilege, resistance, collusion). When we came together each month we explored these ideas through the creative vehicles of poetry, writing, dance, spoken word, theater games, film and visual art. At each meeting, we experientially engaged one or more art forms, reflected on our experiences with these forms and discussed the issues thus raised for understanding race and racism. We came to see this as a collaborative theory building process (Murray, 2006) where we put forth and tested out ideas for understanding and teaching about race and racism through the arts. This collaborative process, described in detail in Bell and Roberts (2010), drew upon the knowledge, expertise and lived experiences of creative team members and used our diverse racial locations and perspectives to create the Storytelling Project Model.

Understanding Race and Racism

Four key interacting concepts undergird how we understand race and racism: race as a social construction, racism as a system that operates on multiple levels, white supremacy/white privilege as key though often neglected aspects of systemic racism, and the problematic notion of color-blindness as an ideal and barrier to racial progress. Our thinking about each of these concepts was influenced by a range of resources and writing that I discuss briefly below.

Race as a Social Construction

We understand race as something that is created through the assumptions, norms and patterns human beings assign to it rather than as a naturally fixed and given category (Omi & Winant, 1986). We recognize that all people are members of a human community that shares the same biological characteristics, exhibiting more variation within so-called racial groups than between groups (Gould, 1996) and that the commonly held concept of different "races" is, in fact, an illusion (Adelman, 2003; Haney-Lopez, 2006). However, we also recognize that the idea of race powerfully shapes the intimately lived experiences of people assigned to various racial categories (Fine, 1997).

> Racial identity is not merely an instrument of rule; it is also an arena and medium of social practice. It is an aspect of individual and collective selfhood. Racial identity in other words does all sorts of practical "work"; it shapes privileged status for some and undermines the social standing of others. It appeals to varied political constituencies, inclusive and exclusive. It codes everyday life in an infinite number of ways. (Winant, 2004, p. 36)

Though constructed through ideas and language, rather than biology, race has significant material consequences in the real world.

Racism as a System that Operates on Multiple Levels

We conceptualize racism as a system of interpersonal, social and institutional patterns and practices that maintain social hierarchies in which Whites as a group benefit at the expense of other groups labeled as "non-white"—African Americans, Latinos, Asian Americans, Native Americans, and Arab Americans (L.A. Bell, 2007; Hardiman & Jackson, 2007). We understand racism as a phenomenon that operates historically to sustain and inform the present, but in ways that often don't leave tracks (Winant, 2004). Because it saturates our institutions and social structures it is like the water in which we swim; the air that we breathe (see Tatum, 2003). It shapes our government, schools, churches, businesses, media and other social institutions in multiple and complex ways that serve to reinforce, sustain and continually reproduce an unequal status quo (Bell, Love & Roberts, 2007). As a system that has been in place for centuries, "business as usual" is sufficient to fuel an institutionalized system of racism that often operates outside of conscious or deliberate intention. Because we must understand its ubiquity in order to effectively challenge its hegemony, the quotidian vehicle of story offers a promising way to get at the commonplace of racism in daily life.

Conscious awareness of racism varies widely among different racial groups, however, and thus shapes the stories to which each group has access (van Dijk, 1999). Whites as a group tend to be less conscious of racism and/or more likely to believe that racism has been addressed than people of color who experience the ongoing effects of racism daily in their lives (L.A. Bell, 2003a; Bonilla-Silva, 2003, 2006a; Myers, 2005; Solorzano, Ceja & Yosso, 2000). Because racial location so powerfully shapes the stories we hear and tell about racism, we thought a great deal about how to account for positionality as we developed the Storytelling Model.

White Supremacy and White Privilege

Race has inescapable material consequences in society, shaping access to resources and life possibilities in ways that benefit the white racial group at the expense of groups of color (Katznelson, 2005; Lipsitz, 2006; Marable, 2002; Massey & Denton, 1993; Oliver & Shapiro, 1997). The racially shaped distribution of resources is illustrated quite powerfully in a DVD we watched and discussed as a creative team in one of our early sessions: "Race: The Power of an Illusion" (Adelman, 2003). This excellent DVD provides a historical and sociological lens for dissecting ideas about race and tracing the consequences of these ideas in American society.

Many recent scholars describe well how whiteness works as the unmarked but presumed norm against which people from other groups are measured (Berger, 1999; Dyer, 1997; Fine, 1997; Frankenberg, 1993, 1997; Hitchcock, 2002; Myers, 2005). Positioning whiteness as a central feature in the study of racism enables us to identify the power dynamics and unearned advantages that accrue to Whites as a group (Frankenberg, 1997; Katznelson, 2005; Kendall, 2006; Lipsitz, 2006; McIntosh, 1990; Oliver & Shapiro, 1997; Wise, 2005). We wanted to unearth stories that expose normative practices that are marked as neutral in order to shine a spotlight on institutions that maintain and bolster white supremacy and to open up analytic possibilities for challenging its hegemony.

Color-Blindness

When Martin Luther King put forth his vision of a color-blind society in his famous "I Have a Dream" speech, he imagined a future where the eradication of racism would eliminate barriers for people of color. He did not mean color-blindness in the naïve sense in which it is so often used today (see for example, Williams, 1998) as signifying "not seeing" skin color. King's vision of a color-blind future in which barriers to children of color are eliminated requires that we see and account for race in order to create institutions and practices that do not replicate patterns of racial inequality that have been rendered as normative. Through a sustained focus on race and racism, the Storytelling Project sought to surface stories that illustrate racism's differential effects on white people and people of color so as to challenge color-blindness and generate more grounded and informed dialogue about racial realities.

Critical Race Theory

We were and continue to be greatly influenced by scholarship in critical race theory (CRT) and its insights about the persistence of racism (D.A. Bell, 1989, 1992; Bell, Delgado & Stefancic, 2005; Delgado & Stefancic, 1995; Matsuda, 1996; Williams, 1991). Like CRT scholars we see race and racism as central to an analysis of inequality, and sustained by stock stories that rationalize the status quo. Like them, we use the idea of counter storytelling to denote stories that counteract or challenge the dominant stories (Delgado, 1989).

However, in our work we differentiate such stories into three types of counter-stories: concealed, resistance and emerging/transforming stories. We conceptualize these story types as pedagogical tools for helping people learn about systemic racism, discern its manifestations in daily life and take action in their own lives to challenge racism and white supremacy. In this way we align with Ladson-Billings' notion of CRT as "an important intellectual and social tool for deconstruction, reconstruction, and construction: deconstruction of oppressive structures and discourses, reconstruction of human agency, and construction of equitable and socially just relations of power" (Ladson-Billings, 2009a, p. 19).

The Power of Storytelling and the Arts

Stories as Analytic Tools

We chose storytelling as a means to explore the topic of racism for several reasons. Stories are one of the most powerful and personal ways that we learn about the world, passed down from generation to generation through the family and cultural groups to which we belong. As human beings we are primed to engage each other and the world through language, and stories can be deeply evocative sources of knowledge and awareness.

Storytelling and oral tradition are also democratic, freely available to all, requiring neither wealth and status nor formal education. Indeed, stories have historically provided ways for people with few material resources to maintain their values and sense of community in the face of forces that would disparage and attempt to destroy them (see for example, Allen, 1992, 1996; Anzaldúa, 2007; Bambara & Morrison, 1996; Dance, 2002; Gwaltney, 1993; Levins Morales, 1998; Silko, 1986; Yosso, 2006).

Because stories operate on both individual and collective levels, they can bridge the sociological, abstract with the psychological, personal contours of daily experience. They help us connect individual experiences with systemic analysis, allowing us to unpack in ways that are perhaps more accessible than abstract analysis alone, racism's hold on us as we move through the institutions and cultural practices that sustain racism. Further, because stories carry within them historical/social formations and sedimented ways of thinking, what Gramsci called "commonsense" (1971), stories offer an accessible vehicle for uncovering normative patterns and historical relations that perpetuate racial privilege. They also potentially enable conscious development of new stories that contest the racial status quo and offer alternative visions for democratic and socially just race relations (Delgado, 1989; Guinier & Torres, 2002).

The Arts as Transformative Learning

Recognizing that racism is "embodied and ideational" as well as "structural and institutional" (Thompson, 1997) the arts provide a way to engage body, heart and mind to open up learning and develop a critical perspective that affords broader understanding of cultural patterns and practices. Sensory engagement without a way to critique social patterns may lead to a myopic focus on individual change that is at best anemic, but intellectual insight into broad patterns without sensory engagement can ultimately be distancing and disempowering. Too often, when we, particularly white people, talk about race we use abstract language, treating racism as something "out there" but not "here" in our daily lives.

The aesthetic experience of stories told through visual arts, theater, spoken word and poetry, can help us think more creatively, intimately and deeply about racism and other challenging social justice issues. The arts provide a realm where charged topics can be encountered and engaged on an embodied level (Roberts, 2005) and thus stimulate deeper learning (Eisner, 2002). Maxine Greene describes this process of engagement thus, "[as] we begin moving between immediacies and general categories...we participate in some dimensions that we could not know if imagination were not aroused" (1995, p. 186).

The arts also unsettle what we take for granted, helping us question normative presumptions about the world so that "commonplaces of racism can be unsettled...rather than taken as natural" (Thompson, 1997). The creative dimensions opened up by aesthetic engagement help us envision new possibilities for challenging and changing oppressive circumstances (Greene, 2004; Roberts, 2005). As Thompson (1997) notes, the arts can "take us up where we are but at the same time shift us, introducing us into new and surprising relationships. No longer grounded in the familiar, we begin to construct fresh understandings, and in the process reconstruct ourselves" (p. 32).

Through helping us to encounter others in more authentic and honest ways the arts may also open up new possibilities for dialogue within and across diverse communities (Clover, 2006; Korza, Schaffer, & Assaf, 2005; Romney, 2005; Soohoo, 2006). Aesthetic experience, and storytelling specifically, create an opening for the teller and listener to "extend, and deepen what each of us thinks of when [we] speak of a community" (Greene, 1995, p. 161) and "provide meaningful examples and ways to identify and connect" (hooks, 1989, p. 77). Through empathic engagement, stories set the stage for affective change; for imagining otherwise (Bruner, 1996; McCrary, 2000; Sarbin, 1986). As we create new narratives we situate ourselves as responsive moral agents, enabling new ways of behaving in line with social justice goals (Wortham, 2000).

Problematizing Story

It is also important to recognize the ways in which the story form can be problematic. The reception and understanding of story depends on context, on the relationship between narrator and listener, on genesis and purpose, on power relations within society (Harris, Carney & Fine, 2001). The diverse groups that make up the United States provide a rich source of stories to draw upon, but in a deeply racialized society stained by structural racism, not all stories are equally acknowledged, affirmed or valued. Vigilance about the danger of story to support an individualistic relativism that elides differences in power and privilege is crucial. Some stories are supported and reinforced by the power structure while others must fight tenaciously to be heard. As hooks comments, "for some, openness is not about the luxury of 'will I choose to share this or tell that' but rather 'will I survive—will I make it through—will I stay alive?'" (1989, p. 2).

All too often discussions of race and racism in the white mainstream, or "whitestream" (Grande, 2004), reify and repeat stock stories developed by the dominant group to put them and their group in a favorable light vis-à-vis others (van Dijk, 1999). Frequently, they are stories of forward racial progress that rationalize white privilege and the status quo (L.A. Bell, 2003a; Bonilla-Silva, Lewis & Embrick, 2004). With awareness, however, such stories can serve as a useful entry point to critically examine race, recognize how racism functions on both individual and systematic levels, and understand its persistence and the factors that enable it to endure (D.A. Bell, 1989).

For people from marginalized communities, stories are a way of bearing witness to their struggle and survival in a racist system (Levins Morales, 1998; Silko, 1986). Such stories persist through tenacious resistance in the face of a status quo that marginalizes and silences their expression, submerging the truths or lessons they impart. Standpoint theory (Hill Collins, 2000) provides a framework for understanding story by highlighting how location in relation to power shapes historically shared, group-based experiences and for acknowledging what is missed when the voices and stories of marginalized people are suppressed or silenced. Critical race theory (Delgado & Stefancic, 1995; Dixson & Rousseau, 2006; Ladson-Billings & Tate, 2006; Matsuda, 1996; Parker & Lynn, 2009; Solarzano & Yosso, 2002) also underscores the value of stories to give voice to the experiences of those oppressed by racism and to provide analytic tools for understanding racism.

For members of the dominant group, critical analysis of stories provides a way to get access to what Anzaldúa (1990) calls "racial blank spots"—the selective editing of reality that allows white people to disengage from the racial advantages we enjoy. If, as Anzaldúa asserts, disengagement is "a sanctioned ethnocentric, racist strategy" then critical engagement with stock and concealed stories offers one way for white people to stay engaged and thus responsive and responsible to racial others.

In the Storytelling Project, we seek ways to identify the conditions necessary for marginalized voices to break through whitestream discourses that silence them, as well as for dominant stories that tell on racism from the inside to be exposed, so as to uncover possibilities for resistance to the racial status quo. We consider ways to create a community in which the often subtle and persistent ways that positionality shapes risk can be noticed and in which differential aspects of story and the connections between individual stories and group experiences with racism can be continually confronted and engaged. We believe that a consciously created counter-storytelling community is the key to the effectiveness of a storytelling methodology designed to confront racism and thus is at the center of the model described below.

The Storytelling Project Model

Creating a Counter-Storytelling Community

At the heart of the Storytelling Project Model is the deliberate creation of a community of diverse members in which stories about race and racism can be openly shared, respectfully heard and critically discussed/analyzed. Many of our early discussions centered on the challenges of establishing a multiracial community of storytellers where issues of social power and privilege can be exposed for critical analysis, dissected and transformed into new imaginaries—i.e. a counter-storytelling community.

Recognizing that people of color tend to bear the weight of talking about race and racism we wanted to find ways to ensure that dominant group members more consciously take on a fair share of this burden. We sought to identify the barriers that so often prevent white people from engaging honestly and responsibly in dialogue about racism. We wanted to invite "kitchen talk...honest, straight up conversation that people have in the kitchen, in contrast to sugar-coated living

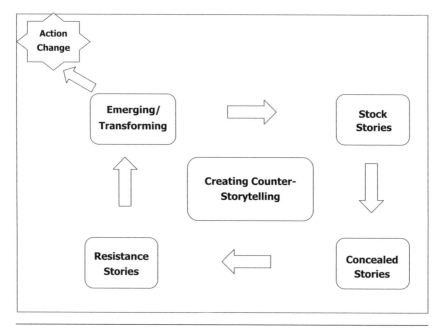

Figure 1.1   The Storytelling Project Model

room conversation that is too polite to get to the heart of the matter" (Korza et al., 2005, p. 108). We experimented with deliberate ways to build community in which color- and power-conscious discussions are invited so that people from different racial locations can better understand their own and others' experiences and the operations of the system that constructs race relations in our society (Frankenberg, 1993; Tatum, 1997).

For counter storytelling in diverse groups to be meaningful and honest we first need to clearly articulate the "terms of engagement" (hooks, 1989). Thus the Storytelling Project Model invites the articulation of ground rules that acknowledge the challenges of recognizing and countering inequality from the different social positions occupied by members of the group. Explicit guidelines can help create a community in which race and racism can be openly discussed, each person's voice and story can be respectfully heard, stories can be held up and scrutinized in terms of their relationship to systems of power and privilege, and practices of power that differentially privilege or mute particular stories (thus reproducing the system we hope to dismantle) can be interrupted. For example, white people are often confronting the realities of racism for the first time, realities that are all too familiar to people of color. Ground rules need to acknowledge these differences and find ways to validate and learn from what different positions/locations teach us about how the system of racism works.

We set forth these intentions with the group and engage them in naming and practicing guidelines that support these intentions so that when conflicts or disagreements arise the guidelines can be used to facilitate thoughtful face-to-face discussion and engagement. While specific guidelines will likely differ from group to group, what matters is that they are intentionally generated to acknowledge differences in power and privilege and to equalize and encourage shared risk-taking. It is also critical that the guidelines be conscientiously used to facilitate honest dialogue and to recognize and stick with uncomfortable moments particularly at the first sign of conflict or disagreement. Establishing such a community is an essential foundation for effectively using the Storytelling Model (see Chapter 6 for a fuller discussion and illustration of the model in practice).

Developing the Story Types

The creative team continually discussed the limitations and opportunities provided by stories to get at what we began to call "the genealogy of racism." We engaged in storytelling, mining our own experiences through writing and poetry and through reading stories and poetry written by others. This process raised provocative questions about the complications of storytelling: stories can be truthful but can also be masks; they can allow us to take on the burdens of racism as well as escape thinking about it; because our identities are multiple our stories also speak to this multiplicity, complicating racism and its intersections with other aspects of social inequality. We found that sometimes telling our stories in the group could help us remember what we had forgotten as individuals about the pains of racism, the rewards of privilege and the normative discourses that make conscious, honest dialogue about racism so difficult to sustain. We grappled with the challenges of using story to unearth socio-cultural practices in a society that valorizes individualism.

Through these conversations we began to differentiate types of stories. The idea of contrasting hegemonic or stock stories with counterstories (L.A. Bell, 2003a) was one starting point. We began to flesh out these two story types in our storytelling experiments. We also looked to history, visual art, poetry and literature for inspiration, as well as to the notion of counter storytelling in critical race theory. These explorations led us to consider and differentiate concealed stories held within oppressed communities that are often hidden or protected from outside scrutiny, as well as to stories of challenge and resistance.

The model we ended up with codifies four story types to describe how people talk and think about race and racism in the United States. These are: stock stories, concealed stories, resistance stories and emerging/transforming stories.[2] As Figure 1.1 shows, building a counterstorytelling community is central to exploring the four story types. We conceive of these stories as connected and mutually interacting. Each story type leads into the next in a cycle that fills out and expands our understanding of and ability to creatively challenge racism. The story types provide language and a framework for making sense of race and racism through exploring the genealogy of racism and the social stories that generate and reproduce it through the stock stories that keep it in place.

Stock stories are introduced as the first type because they are the most public and ubiquitous in the mainstream institutions of society—schools, businesses, government and the media—and because the other story types, as counter-stories, critique and challenge the presumption of universality in stock stories. Thus, they provide the ground against which we build our analysis. Stock stories are the tales told by the dominant group, passed on through historical and literary documents, and celebrated through public rituals, law, the arts, education and media. Because stock stories tell a great deal about what a society considers important and meaningful, they provide a useful starting point for analyzing how racism operates to valorize and advantage the dominant white group.

For example, we examine stock stories about the American Dream through poetry, political speeches, songs and public art that delineate aspects of this iconic story—individualism, meritocracy and inevitable forward progress presumed for any person who works hard to get ahead. We analyze these stories so as to expose and question their presumed normative status and to question what they leave out (see Chapter 2).

Concealed stories coexist alongside the stock stories but most often remain in the shadows, hidden from mainstream view, but provide a perspective that is often very different from that of the mainstream (Scott, 1990). Concealed stories reveal both the hidden (from the mainstream) stories told from the perspective of racially dominated groups, as well as stories uncovered through critical analysis of historical and social science data that illustrate how race shapes experience in our society. Though invisible to those in the mainstream, concealed stories are circulated, told and retold by people in the margins whose experiences and aspirations they express and honor (Levins Morales, 1998). Through concealed stories people who are marginalized, and often stigmatized, by the dominant society recount their experiences and critique or "talk back" to mainstream narratives, portraying the strengths and capacities within marginalized communities, what Yosso (2006) calls "community cultural wealth." Levins Morales writes, "We must struggle to re-create the shattered knowledge of our humanity. It is in retelling stories of victimization, recasting our roles from subhuman scapegoats to beings full of dignity and courage, that this becomes possible" (1998, p. 13).

Following the lead of critical race theory, which underlines the value of experiential knowledge about race and racism, we begin with activities that tell the stories of racial oppression through the experiences of people of color. These stories tend to narrate the past and ongoing realities of racism that are either invisible or only glimpsed in the stock stories. For example, we examine poetry and art created by artists from marginalized communities that describe the realities of working hard but never getting ahead, of striving to realize the American Dream but continually facing barriers to progress. We also search for the stories concealed in statistics and social science data about the racial distribution of life opportunities and access.

Such stories guide the search for concealed structures of racial inequality and the hidden stories of normalized white advantage. Through contrasting stock and concealed stories we develop analytic tools to examine the concealed stories that reveal the underside of racism and use these tools to identify the hidden advantages for Whites and penalties for people of color. We explore such questions as: What are the stories about race and racism that we don't hear? Why don't we hear them? How are such stories lost/left out? How do we recover these stories? What do these stories show us about racism that the stock stories do not?

While concealed stories are often eclipsed by stock stories, they are everywhere to be excavated and held up to the stock stories they challenge. We deconstruct stock stories through comparing them to concealed stories, identifying different perspectives and knowledge, and developing a fuller picture of our society and its institutions. Such comparisons help us understand how stock stories maintain the institutional and social status quo in ways that scaffold and perpetuate a racial system that ultimately harms everyone by preventing realization of our democratic ideals (see Chapter 3).

Resistance stories are the third type of story we examine in the model. These are the warehouse of stories that demonstrate how people have resisted racism, challenged the stock stories that support it, and fought for more equal and inclusive social arrangements through-out our history but seldom taught in our schools. Resistance stories include the reserve of stories accumulated over time about and by peo-ple and groups who have challenged an unjust racial status quo. They include stories of "sheroes" and "heroes" who have been excluded (and sometimes included and vilified) in history books, but who have nev-ertheless struggled against racism. Too often we simplify resistance through iconic stories of heroic individuals that sanitize the collec-tive struggles that drive social change, and thus fail to pass on neces-sary lessons about how social change actually comes about (Menkart, Murray & View, 2004). Resistance stories teach about antiracist per-spectives and practices that have existed throughout our history up to the present time to expand our vision of what is possible in our own antiracism work today.

Resistance stories serve as guides and inspiration for the hard work ahead. They provide tools and examples of ways to resist and work against racism and imagine possibilities for resisting the racial status quo. Guiding questions for discovering/uncovering resistance stories include: What stories exist (historical or contemporary) that serve as examples of resistance? What role does resistance play in challenging the stock stories about racism? What can we learn about antiracist action and perseverance against the odds by looking at these stories?

Finally, we explore **emerging/transforming stories**. These coun-ter-stories are new stories deliberately constructed to challenge the stock stories, build on and amplify concealed and resistance stories, and create new stories to interrupt the status quo and energize change. Such stories enact continuing critique and resistance to the stock sto-ries, subvert taken for granted racial patterns and enable imagination of new possibilities for inclusive human community. In sharp contrast to naïve, ahistorical stories, they are grounded in and emerge from a critical analysis of stock and concealed stories that reveal social pat-terns. The analysis is further developed through resistance stories that provide models for generating new stories that imagine alternative scenarios for racial equality and articulate strategies to work toward these visions.

Guiding questions include: What would it look like if we trans-formed the stock stories? What can we draw from resistance stories to create new stories about what ought to be? What kinds of communities based on justice can we imagine and then work to enact? What kinds of stories can support our ability to speak out and act where instances of racism occur? (See Chapters 4 and 5.)

These four story types are intricately connected. Stock stories and concealed stories are in effect two sides of the same coin, reflecting on the same "realities" of social life, but from quite different positions and perspectives. Resistance and emerging/transforming stories are also linked through their capacity to challenge the stock stories. Resistance stories become the base upon which emerging/transforming stories can be imagined and serve to energize their creation. Emerging/transforming stories then build anew in each generation as people engage with the struggles before them and learn from and build on the resistance stories that preceded them.

The model also recognizes the persistence of racism and the possibility of recruitment and cooptation back into the status quo as racism shape-shifts to appear in new forms. In the model (see Figure 1.1), arrows show the potential for moving outward toward action and change, but also back toward stock stories. These possible directions indicate the need to stay mindful and open to new stories as we continue to learn about racism and its effects on diverse communities.

The act of placing diverse stories side by side as worthy of critical inspection enables us to see that the mainstream story is not normative but one among many, and thus contestable. We learn to attend to stories from the margins as sources of crucial information our society needs if we are to realize our democratic ideals. In this way, the Storytelling Project Model provides tools for developing a critical lens that can be applied to many areas of analysis and thus engage people in critical learning for social justice.

We are convinced that the Storytelling Project Model and the story types we identify present a powerful pedagogical framework for helping people develop a critical understanding of race and racism. We have developed a curriculum based on the model (Bell, Roberts, Irani & Murphy, 2008) and followed its use in two high school classrooms (see Chapter 4). The students who participated in the experimental implementation of this curriculum found the model to be a meaningful framework for analyzing race and racism in their school and community and for generating alternatives for change (Roberts, Bell & Murphy, 2008). We have also used the model for in-service teacher education and teacher professional development (see Chapters 5 and 6). The teachers who participated in our summer institute in 2005 described it as an "innovative and powerful" means for raising and looking at issues of race and racism in their classrooms (see Chapter 6). We plan to develop the model further by exploring its usefulness for examining other social justice issues.

Conclusion

The Storytelling Project Model asks those who use it to consider what we lose when stories of and by diverse groups are concealed or lost, and what we gain as a society when we listen to and learn from the multitude of stories available for our consideration as we seek to dismantle racist structures and patterns in our society. It invites people to tell their own stories and through such telling envision a future that embraces inclusion, equity and justice for all of the diverse people in our country. As Martin Luther King reminds us, "We are in an inescapable network of mutuality, tied in a single garment of destiny. Whatever affects one directly, affects all indirectly" (quoted in Barlow, 2003). It is our hope that the ongoing examination and construction of such stories can be powerful tools for motivating and sustaining antiracist work and generating democratic change.

The following chapters illustrate the Storytelling Project Model through several iterations and examples in practice. Each chapter highlights a different story type, examining that story type in depth and showing how it links to other parts of the model. Each also explores applications of the model and further draws out the role of storytelling and the arts in developing our understanding of race and racism.

2

STOCK STORIES

Reproducing Racism and White Advantage

History runs thick in all of us.

(Carroll, 1997)

This chapter introduces the first story type in the Storytelling Project Model—*stock stories*. Here I define stock stories and examine the functions they serve, illustrating how stock stories operate in everyday talk to legitimize the perspectives of the dominant white racial group in our society. Next I hone in on one example of an iconic stock story—the American Dream. I describe one of the activities we use in the Storytelling Project to critically analyze the American Dream and illustrate how stock stories can be explored through art-based activities.

Stock stories are a set of standard, typical or familiar stories held in reserve to explain racial dynamics in ways that support the status quo, like a supply of goods kept on the premises to be pulled out whenever the necessity calls for a ready response. As "canned" stories they are stale and predictable, but they have a long shelf-life. They preclude originality, immediacy or surprise that fresh, unscripted, potentially uncomfortable stories or encounters might open up about racial/social life in the United States and thus about how we understand racial patterns and the dynamics that sustain them.

The term "stock" also connotes a share in capital that investors reap from owning stock in companies. Just so, Whites are invested in stock stories that flatter and support our social position, providing shares in the racial status quo. We inherit these assets accumulated across a history of special advantages, but tend to assume them as our birthright and perhaps the earned rewards for our unique capacities as individuals, failing to recognize the racialized system that awarded them and the unfair social and material benefits they perpetuate.

Stock has a third connotation with ancestry, often with reference to race or ethnic group. Stock stories affirm, albeit often unconsciously and obliquely, the superiority of the stock of whiteness. As the group defined as normal, "white" stock is presumed to be proper, desired, the taken for granted way things are meant to be. In all of these senses, stock stories operate to confirm and benefit Whites as the "natural" and deserving beneficiaries of the racial status quo in the United States.

Though mediated by class, gender, age, sexual orientation and other factors, whiteness accrues benefits (legitimacy, respect, opportunity, protection) not available to people of color. For example, a poor white woman may not have the same amount of racial privilege as a wealthy white man, but the meager amount she does have provides benefits, however small, over a woman of color in the same circumstances, and often over persons of color of any means. That such advantage exists, even in the face of great inequality among Whites, is evident in the history of poor and working-class Whites who, against their own economic self-interest, have rejected coalitions with similarly situated people of color (Kelley, 1996).

Stock Stories Are Collective But Speak through Individuals

It is hardly surprising in a racially diverse society that people from different groups think and talk about one another and generate stories to explain our interactions (Smitherman & van Dijk, 1988; van Dijk, 1984, 1993, 1999). Yet such stories are not simply personal or idiosyncratic but are produced and communicated within specific historical contexts and social locations that shape their meaning—the stories we tell are those that are available for the telling (Ewick & Silbey, 1995). Ideas about race reverberate, often unconsciously, through individual stories in ways that reinforce and legitimize broad social patterns— history indeed "runs thick in all of us."

A recent poll reveals that the majority of white Americans believe that racism is no longer a major obstacle to advancement for African Americans and other people of color, often asserting that we are in a "post-racial," color-blind era and have moved "beyond race" (Herring, 2006; Sack, 2008). These beliefs echo an emblematic stock story of America as a "color-blind" meritocracy where opportunity is open to anyone who works hard enough to achieve their goals. This is the story my mother passed on to me in quite explicit language and is one that is shared by many others in this society.

I grew up in the 1950s, in the middle of Indiana, in the middle of the country, in a General Motors town enjoying the employment boom of car-obsessed culture. Like many places in the U.S. then and now, the town was racially diverse but residentially segregated. The only high school in town at the time was also racially diverse but, as I understand looking back now, academically segregated through tracking. My mother, a divorced parent of three children and "dyed-in-the-wool Democrat," taught us a fervent belief in American democracy, meritocracy and opportunity—espousing the ideas of Ayn Rand and Norman Vincent Peale among others—alongside a liberal color-blindness that said we should not see color and should treat everyone the same. The racial epithets we heard from other white people were considered "trashy" and we were not allowed to talk that way. These ideals and injunctions operated alongside passivity in the face of neighbors and others who actively expressed racist sentiments and, as we grew older, anxious concern when my siblings and I invited home black friends.

This stock story supports the idea that, despite slavery and other shameful periods in our history, the country has moved forward and no longer has the responsibility to actively right wrongs of the past. Indeed, many Whites suggest that we need to "get past" race and even fault those who continue to bring up issues of discrimination as the real cause of the problem (L.A. Bell, 2003a; Bonilla-Silva, Lewis & Embrick, 2004; Bush, 2004). From this perspective, patience prevails over urgency in addressing racial inequalities that persist, complacently trusting that racism will be rectified in due time.

In contrast, stories told by people of color more often reflect awareness of past and continuing discrimination in most aspects of life, and an understanding that while our history oscillates between cycles of progress and retreat on racial matters, ongoing inequality tenaciously persists (D.A. Bell, 1992; Feagin & Sikes, 1994; Frankenberg, 1993; Hacker, 1995; Hochschild, 1995; Shipler, 1997). Like other

Americans, people of color embrace the American Dream and the ideal of working hard to get ahead, but see this possibility thwarted by continuing racial barriers (Cose, 1995; Hochschild, 1995). Frustration with the slow pace of change and anger at what they see as inevitable retreat are the understandable response. Journalist Ellis Cose captures this perception gap, "Built into almost every interaction between blacks [and other people of color] and whites is the entire history of race relations in America" (Cose, 1997, p. 185).

Without accounting for the history of race relations in our country and the ongoing reverberations today, we are unable to see or understand the patterns that sustain racial hierarchy and inequality.

> Our public and private talk about race is often ambivalent and confused because the lenses through which we view it are partial, in both senses of the word. It's like trying to take a picture of a large, heterogeneous crowd with a Polaroid; we get snapshots of individuals frozen in time, lacking the depth of field to show their relationship to each other, their social environment, and their histories. (Peck, 1994, p. 114)

It is these interlocking relationships and histories that we seek to expose through looking critically at stock stories. The transformative value of learning the history of racism in this country came home to me when I encountered African American history in college.

> *In college I encountered for the first time knowledge, opinions and world-views that radically challenged everything I had previously learned in my family and at school. As a history major I enrolled in a course in African American History, and eventually double majored in History and Afro-American Studies. Exposure to a history I had never been taught opened up a whole new world, radically upending the stock stories I had grown up with about democracy, meritocracy, fairness, equality and my benign place in the world. Stunned that I could be so ignorant, I began to question everything and to take a much more critical view of my country, its espoused ideals and the trustworthiness of my own experience as a measure of reality.*

Historical knowledge enables one to discern patterns in society that shape racial position and opportunity so as to understand the systematic nature of racism and challenge the stock stories that support it.

Stock Stories Are Not Innocent

Stock stories about race are strategic, operating to advance particular goals and interests (Bonilla-Silva, 2006b; van Dijk, 1984; Wetherell & Potter, 1992). For example, white talk about "minorities" often serves to confirm dominant group perceptions and present white people in a favorable light by comparison (L.A. Bell, 2003a; Bonilla-Silva, 2006a; van Dijk, 1993, 1999). Stock stories operate as "socially shared tales that incorporate a common scheme and wording...and provide ideological support for white dominance" (Bonilla-Silva et al., 2004). Examples include arguments that since white people today did not own slaves we are not responsible for sins of long ago; after all "the past is the past." Some even assert that we have gone too far and that now the problem is "reverse racism." Such thinking is captured in numerous interviews with white people in the United States and in Europe (L.A. Bell, 2003a; Bonilla-Silva, 2006a; Bush, 2004; Cobas & Feagin, 2007; Frankenberg, 1993; Gutiérrez-Jones, 2001; McKinney, 2005; van Dijk, 1993).

Stock stories personalize story lines about other groups, creating a "social data base" or stockpile of stories individual Whites can draw on to explain social reality. These "testimonials" provide "an aura of authenticity" (Bonilla-Silva et al., 2004) when familiar stories about racial others are retold as if the narrator had experienced such encounters first hand. Often stories challenging Affirmative Action are of this ilk—stories of a friend or family member who did not get a job that was given to a "less-qualified" minority. Such stories are inevitably biased since they are second or third hand and the speaker is rarely privy to the actual qualifications and considerations of the parties involved. Or they are stories that focus on "quotas" or "preferences" with no acknowledgment of the historically stacked deck in favor of white people that created the need in the first place for affirmative or proactive action to pry open opportunity systematically denied to others.

Van Dijk speculates that stock stories allow Whites to draw upon negative stereotypes and complain about other groups without being subject to charges of racism themselves. Such stories ignore or minimize the ways in which past inequality continues to play out in our present economic and social structure, support assertions that our society is "color-blind" or "race neutral," and perpetuate the notion that anyone can advance based on individual merit. Such stories became familiar to me when I first started teaching in a predominantly black middle school and continually heard these ideas in the comments of white colleagues and friends.

> *As a young teacher in a northeastern urban school district, I witnessed daily the disconnect between the incredible efforts my students and their families made in the face of obstacles and realities with which they had to contend, and the disparaging views of white friends and colleagues about them. I had constant arguments with well-meaning white people who assume without question that they have earned what they have through hard work and that those who have not succeeded, particularly people of color, are lazy or lacking in gumption or simply incapable of doing what is necessary to pull themselves up by their bootstraps. If only they had our "values" and "work ethic."*

Through deconstructing stock stories we see that there is something at stake in the stories we tell. Stock stories not only legitimize a flattering self-portrait of the dominant white racial group, but in retelling contribute to their ongoing reproduction (Ewick & Silbey, 1995; Scott, 1990). For example, the story of meritocracy affirms an image of fairness and justifies positions of dominance as rightly earned, while simultaneously holding those who are not successful accountable for their own failure. This stock story creates a vicious cycle of "blaming the victim" that justifies and perpetuates systemic racism (Hochschild, 1995; Ryan, 1976).

Maintaining white dominance in the face of counteracting evidence, however, requires continual reiteration and confirmation. "Finding expression and being refashioned within the stories of countless individuals may lead to a polyvocality that inoculates and protects the master narrative from critique" (Ewick & Silbey, 1995, p. 212). Thus focusing a critical spotlight on everyday stories may be a crucial place to intervene and expose master narratives that sustain racism.

Stock Stories Neutralize Challenges to Their Authority

Stock stories not only teach what we should assume as truth, they also warn of the consequences of nonconformity and preempt alternative stories that might challenge their veracity (Ewick & Silbey, 1995). Those who contradict dominant narratives often encounter shocked disbelief in the face of what is taken as their self-evident validity. Individuals, from any racial group, who assert counter-narratives that challenge stock stories are met with ridicule, ignored or dismissed as fringe or crazy. I am reminded of this in an experience I had as a new faculty member.

> *I am in a meeting with the administrators at my college and some other faculty (all-white) following a racial incident on our campus. Elderhostel guests (white) living in a summer dorm have complained that the students (of color) next door are playing their radio too loud. Campus police (white) arrive and rudely challenge the students using abusive language and in one reported instance blow cigar smoke in a student's face. The argument escalates, town police arrive, and four students, including our current student body president, are taken to jail. The students call the director of student affairs for help but rather than bailing them out, he leaves them in jail overnight. Their understandable outrage and sense of betrayal leads to defiance and demonstrations as more students (and some faculty/staff) join them.*
>
> *Our meeting is to address this problem. I suggest that we need to consider the issue of racism on campus and question our own unacknowledged racial blindness. They look at me as if I have three heads. "We're not racist! How dare you say such a thing!" I try to explain that I'm not judging them—I include myself in this analysis—but merely arguing that we try to see things from the perspective of the students and try to understand how we may be operating on racist assumptions of which we are not even aware. With every word, I can see that I am becoming more and more alien, irrational, crazy. I am quickly pushed to the margin of this conversation, someone to be dismissed, as my colleagues of color were before the conversation even began.*

While both white people and people of color are familiar with the stock stories regarding race, Whites as the dominant group are much less likely to be aware of the contradicting stories that circulate within communities of color. Thus white people are often taken by surprise when confronted with alternative scenarios and interpretations of racial experience, as my colleagues above were and as were many who listened to Senator Obama's speech on race and even more so to the excerpts of sermons by the minister of his church, Reverend Wright.

Stock stories become an effective strategy for marginalizing social and political claims by people of color and neutralizing potential challenges to the racial status quo (D. Bell, 2009; Doane & Bonilla-Silva, 2003). For example, despite ample evidence to the contrary, stock stories portray integration as an achieved fact, asserting that we are a color-blind, even "post-racial" society. Journalist Ellis Cose explains this as a "perception gap [that] quietly shapes how blacks and whites interpret the world, their experiences and each other. It shows up in our assumptions and rationalizations, in our decisions and politics, in our neighborhoods and schools. To be sure not all whites think alike about race, nor do all blacks. But the consensus within each race is striking" (Cose, 1997, p. 193). This perception gap exists between Whites and other groups of color as well.

The "integration illusion" appears impervious to abundant social science data and stories emerging from the lived experiences of people of color that point to quite a different reality. Schooling, housing, employment, social relations, religious observation, the media, relations with police, literally every area of social life, are experienced differently by Whites and people of color (Isaacs, 2007; Lipsitz, 2006; Oliver & Shapiro, 1997; Steinhorn & Diggs-Brown, 1999). Stock stories neutralize and defuse such counter-claims and contradictory evidence.

Stock Stories Are Not Immutable

Still, stock stories do not go unchallenged. Alternative stories find voice in the counter-narratives of people of color and white "racial progressives" (Bonilla-Silva et al., 2004) who defy the status quo and insist on other versions of reality. Communities of color have always nurtured stories that testify to their realities and experiences with racism. White people can also develop a consciousness that acknowledges our ties to a racist history and expose how racism is learned and enacted among Whites from an insider perspective (Alcoff, 1998).

I am grateful to the historical examples of Whites who challenged racism and to the African American History classes that introduced me to these early abolitionists. I have spent a good part of my adult life trying to understand the forces that maintain the gap between our national rhetoric of equality and realities on the ground. As an insider to white culture, I know intimately the stories, rationalizations, and resistances to acknowledging racism. I also feel the powerful tug of conformity to a status quo from which I benefit as a result of white advantage. I recognize that understanding my racial location is key to my evolving consciousness, excavating my blind spots, and developing the ongoing commitment to listen to, learn from and build bridges with people of color to collaborate in dismantling racism. I recognize that this work is ongoing and never complete and that I am constantly being recruited back into the stock stories I resist.

Stock stories can thus be destabilized through stories that voice the knowledge generated within communities of color and among white antiracists.

American Dream/American Realities

The American Dream, the assertion that anyone who works hard enough can get ahead, is familiar to everyone in this country, including our newest immigrants. As the story goes, in America, unlike societies where title and inherited wealth determine life chances and opportunities, individuals can pull themselves up by their own bootstraps and, with enough hard work and fortitude, ensure their own children will be better off than those of previous generations. This optimistic assertion that personal opportunity is available to all is one of the most deeply held tenets of American life (Bullock & Lott, 2006; Kluegel & Smith, 1986).

The centrality of this iconic stock story is evident in the frequency with which presidents and politicians invoke it in their speeches; its durability evident in the way it is so broadly embraced, even by those whose lives do not realize its promises. People of color as much as white people, poor people as much as the affluent, aspire to the American Dream in their own lives (Hochschild, 1995). In fact, the least enfranchised are often the most faithful to its tenets, shown by their hard work and perseverance in the face of, often insurmountable, obstacles. They also are more likely to see the barriers to attaining the Dream and to be more critical of platitudes about meritocracy and individual opportunity.

Whites believe the American Dream works for everyone; blacks believe it only works for those not of their race. Whites are angry that blacks refuse to see the openness and fairness of the system; blacks are angry that whites refuse to see the biases and blockages in the system. If this disparity worsens the American dream cannot maintain its role as the central organizing belief of all Americans. (Hochschild, 1995, p. 68)

Hochschild argues further that, "the ideology of the American Dream forecloses empathy for the plight of those who fail to reach it, ensuring that others will see them as losers" (p. 34). The stock story of the American Dream thus sets up a vicious cycle where barriers of race and class make it likely that certain people "are disproportionately likely to fail to achieve their goals...and are [then] blamed as individuals (and perhaps blame themselves) for their failure...carry[ing] the further stigma as members of non-virtuous (thus appropriately denigrated) groups" (Hochschild, 1995, p. 34).

While the lives of African Americans and other people of color have clearly improved over the past forty years (in terms of access to jobs, gains in education and participation in politics, for example), the concealed stories embedded in social science data reveal the distortions and traps in the American Dream stock story. For example, recent economic analyses show a huge and compounding discrepancy between the ability of Whites to accumulate and transfer assets to the next generation and that of other groups; while ongoing unemployment, underemployment, racial segregation in jobs and discrimination in hiring and promotion create a permanent recession for people of color (Center, 2009; Isaacs, 2007; Oliver & Shapiro, 1997). While some gains can be seen in health indicators, the death rate for Blacks and Latinos is higher than for Whites and the diseases they suffer are less likely to be addressed by medical research (Sack, 2008). If we look at home ownership, while Blacks have made progress, "a smaller fraction of Blacks own their own homes in 1990 than did Whites in 1920" (Hochschild, 1995, p. 47). On average, homes owned by Blacks hold barely more than half the value of homes owned by Whites, and the recent sub-prime mortgage scandal has made these disparities far worse (Center, 2009). If we look at residential integration, "Blacks remain much more highly segregated than Asians or Latinos and are less likely to live in suburbs" (Center, 2009, p. 41; see also Massey & Denton, 1993).

Despite overwhelming evidence of these gaps, Whites continue to minimize racism and assert color-blind, post-racial ideologies. "African Americans increasingly believe that racial discrimination is worsening and that it inhibits their race's ability to participate in the American dream; whites increasingly believe that discrimination is lessening and that blacks have the same chance to participate in the dream as whites" (Hochschild, 1995, p. 55). This discrepancy fuels divisions and foments white resistance to the remedies needed to create the opportunities espoused in the Dream, thus perpetuating the status quo.

Unpacking the American Dream: An Example

Poetry, political speeches, history and other narratives can be used to engage people in complicating and deconstructing the stock story of the American Dream. One activity we devised draws on the oratory of two politicians: Arnold Schwarzenegger and Barack Obama as they addressed the presidential conventions of their respective parties in 2004. We have used this lesson with high school students, with higher education professionals at national conferences, and with undergraduates preparing to become teachers.

Participants divide into small "same-speech" groups of four or five per group. Each group receives copies of one of the two speeches—half of the groups read the Obama speech and half read the Schwarzenegger speech. Abridged copies of the speeches are available in the Storytelling Project Curriculum at http://www.barnard.edu/education/grants_projects.php. High school students especially love reading the Schwarzenegger speech using the accent and swagger from his movie persona. After reading their assigned speech, group members identify and categorize references to the American Dream found in their speech.

Both speeches repeatedly talk about the American Dream and share many of the same images and assumptions about it. For example, Schwarzenegger says, "To think that a once scrawny boy from Austria could grow up to become governor of California and stand in Madison Square Garden to speak on behalf of the president of the United States, that is an immigrant's dream. It is the American Dream." Obama invokes similar sentiments in his speech, "I stand here knowing that my story is part of the larger American story, that I owe a debt to all of those who came before me, and that, in no other country on earth, is my story even possible."

Next we remix the groups in jigsaw fashion to form new groups of members who have read both speeches. Together these "mixed-speech" groups create a Venn diagram—two overlapping circles in which one circle represents the Obama speech and the other represents the Schwarzenegger speech (see Figure 2.1). Drawing on their lists from the same-speech groups, participants categorize references to the American Dream made by each politician into the Obama circle, the Schwarzenegger circle or, in the case of shared references, in the space where the circles overlap. For example, the quotes noted above suggest that in the overlapping circle both men invoke their own story to show that the American Dream works. Items in the Schwarzenegger circle might include: Republican, language no barrier, limited role for government, John Wayne as hero—rugged individualism. In the Obama circle might be: Democrat, more work needs to be done, the dream not yet complete, need for government change in priorities, our connections to each other.

In the following discussion, each group presents to the whole group the Venn diagram they have created. We find that typically the analysis is consistent across groups. Usually all groups describe similarities where ideas about the American Dream overlap and important key differences in the two speeches. We consider the area of overlap to be the heart of the stock story of the American Dream. The circles where the politicians diverge we view as liberal and conservative versions of the American Dream stock story. Taken as a whole they illustrate the power and pervasiveness of this stock story across ideology and political position.

We then ask groups to consider what is outside of the Venn diagram altogether. What is in neither circle? Who is not included? What stories are left out? What is not mentioned at all? What is invisible? What cannot be said? This is where concealed stories may be found that can help us look at the American Dream from a different angle.

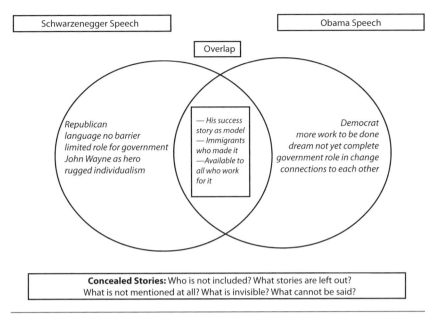

Figure 2.1   Venn Diagram: The American Dream Stock Story

This activity motivates a critical view of stock stories and initiates a search for concealed stories to discover what they reveal about the American Dream that the stock story does not.

African American poet Langston Hughes vividly evokes what happens to those who faithfully embrace the Dream but are continually thwarted from receiving its promised rewards in his poem, "A Dream Deferred." This poem can be another focus for engaging in the analytic process described above. Hughes captures a yearning for the American Dream, a willingness to work hard for it, as well as the anger and bitterness engendered when its promise is continually postponed—"maybe it just sags like a heavy load, or does it explode?" Held up as a contrast to the stock story, the poem provokes us to consider: What would need to happen for the American Dream to truly work for everyone in this society? What would need to change? The next chapter takes up and explores concealed stories and illustrates further how the juxtaposition of stock and concealed stories can be used to support greater understanding and more critical analysis of stories and social patterns that perpetuate racism.

3

CONCEALED STORIES

Reclaiming Subjugated Memory and Knowledge

> History is the struggle over who has the authority to tell the stories that define us.
>
> **(Levins Morales, 1998, p. 5)**

Persevering in the shadows of stock stories are **concealed stories**, the second story type explored in the Storytelling Project Model. While stock stories offer the sanitized official version at the center of public life, concealed stories embody the teeming, unruly and contradictory stories that leak out from the margins. These are stories about racial experience eclipsed by stock stories that colonize the limelight. While stock stories control mainstream discourse and naturalize white racial dominance, concealed stories narrate the ways that race differentially shapes life experiences and opportunities, disputing the unblemished tales of color-blindness, opportunity and laudatory progress propagated by stock stories.

Like stock stories, concealed stories are not purely individual but rather connect to broad social and historical patterns. Concealed stories about experiences with racism link back to the historical relations and social policies that produce them—and can never be solely understood as individual. This is an important distinction in a talk show-saturated culture where the individual and idiosyncratic are so pervasively valorized. The popular usage of story works counter to the project of this book where I want to focus on the patterned threads that connect stories to social practices in order to understand the persistence of racism.

The Storytelling Project creative team very consciously chose the term concealed to signify that these stories are just beneath the surface;

not so much unknown as constantly overshadowed, pushed back into the margins, conveniently "forgotten" or repressed. Like unwelcome company, concealed stories disconcert stock stories, challenging their smug complacency and assumed normality by insisting on a different accounting of experience. Through alternative renderings of the lived experiences of racial subordination and racial advantage, concealed stories present a more encompassing view of reality, one that exposes the partiality and self-interest in stock stories.

Concealed stories challenge stock stories by offering different accounts of and explanations for social relations. In the face of stock stories that insist otherwise, they "name and reclaim, over and over, the connections we are taught to ignore, the dynamics we are told do not exist" (Levins Morales, 1998, pp. 4–5). Such counter-stories can be narrated by both white people and people of color but, because of how we are situated as narrators in a hierarchical racial system, they tend to comment on different aspects of the system of racism. Concealed stories by people of color tell about how racism is experienced by those subjected to racism and, for reasons of safety and survival, are often told outside of the hearing of the dominant group (Scott, 1990). This "subjugated knowledge" (Hill Collins, 2000) offers firsthand evidence of the impact of discrimination on those at the receiving end of racialized policies and practices. These stories also catalogue "community cultural wealth" (Yosso, 2006), the strengths, capacities and resilience within marginalized communities that are invisible, ignored or trivialized in stock stories.

Concealed stories are embodied in the everyday talk of people on the margins as they articulate their experiences, the challenges they face, the struggles to make it, and their aspirations and despairs living with the burdens of racism (see for example, Anzaldúa, 1990; D.A. Bell, 1989, 1992; Bonilla-Silva, 2001; Carroll, 1997; Collier-Thomas & Franklin, 2001; Deloria, 1995; Essed, 1991; Gwaltney, 1993; Kitwana, 2002; Levins Morales, 1998; Marable, 2002; Matsuda, 1996; Williams, 1991). Such stories are shared in church basements, bars, street corners and front porches—everywhere that those beaten down by racism gather to let down their burdens and renew themselves for another day. The stories thread through family narratives and traditions. They are embedded in the everyday speech of young people and elders, as well as in the oratory of politicians and reformers. Concealed stories are found in poetry, art, dance, music and drama that creatively express the trauma of being dehumanized by racism as well as the hard-won knowledge, wisdom and strength to carry on in the face of injustice.

Concealed stories can also be discovered in the stories of white people who have become conscious of racism's effects and expose how whiteness is taught and learned as an ideology of dominance. Such stories "tell on" racism (L.A. Bell, 2003a), revealing how racism is learned and reinforced within white communities, thus exposing from the inside the dynamics of how privilege is reproduced. Such stories are available from white antiracists who provide an insider perspective on socialization and conditioning in white society (see for example, Adelman, 2003; L.A. Bell, 2003a; Berger, 1999; Bush, 2004; Fine, 1997; Frankenberg, 1993; Kendall, 2006; Kivel, 1996; Lewis, 2003; Lipsitz, 2006; McIntosh, 1990; McKinney, 2005; Roy, 1999; Smith, 2007; Wise, 2005). Though much less ubiquitous, they can be also found in literature and the arts, music and poetry, history and everyday talk by white people who honestly examine and critique their location in a racist society. These stories of and by "race traitors" (Garvey & Ignatiev, 1996) subvert norms of complicity with business as usual and open the way for white people to create more inclusive and authentic relationships with people of color, relationships that can sustain alliances to work against racism (Kendall, 2006).

Mainstream discourse, however, works against the telling and hearing of concealed stories that challenge dominant white racial views of the world. For example, media furor over Reverend Jeremiah Wright's sermons reflected the lack of awareness among the white majority of concealed stories so familiar in communities of color. Listeners of color, whether or not they agreed with Reverend Wright's views, were not surprised by either his rhetoric or critique of U.S. policy in a 2003 sermon describing his reading of the gospels and the treatment of black Americans. This segment was played endlessly in the media accompanied by shocked and outraged commentary about his inflammatory words.

The government gives them drugs, builds bigger prisons, passes a three-strike law, and then wants us to sing "God Bless America." No, no, no, God damn America, that's in the Bible for killing innocent people...God damn America for treating our citizens as less than human, God damn America for as long as she acts like she is God and she is supreme.

Those familiar with a historical discourse tradition of taking America to task for its failure to address the oppression of black people were not surprised, but such alternative discourses and perspectives on the operations of power are typically invisible in the mainstream, and for many Whites came as a complete shock. In the absence of critical commentary that would open up understanding through connecting historical and contemporary patterns in race relations, they were incapable of considering the legitimate historical grievances alluded to in the speech.

Candidate Obama's speech on race in Philadelphia attempted to highlight and explain these links to history and racial location: "We do not need to recite here the history of racial injustice in this country. But we do need to remind ourselves that so many of the disparities that exist in the African-American community today can be directly traced to inequalities passed on from an earlier generation that suffered under the brutal legacy of slavery and Jim Crow" (Obama, 2008). He goes on to trace many of these patterns from segregated schools to inferior schooling for students of color today, from legalized discrimination in housing, lending, unions and employment to the wealth and income gaps and disproportionate poverty rates we see today.

Such connections are critical for understanding racism and the differential ways Whites and people of color recall the past and understand the present. Tracing the patterns that connect helps us see that memory is as much social as personal, shaped by the contexts that elicit and give it meaning (Apfelbaum, 2000; Griffin, 2004). The social function of memory is evident in official representations and interpretations of the past (historical memory) that preserve what is to be memorialized and celebrated, and by omission, what is to be ignored and trivialized, thus privileging some stories over others. Through such renderings, the history presented by the dominant group is made to "seem transparent" and thus uncontestable, making it difficult for aggrieved communities to get their claims for justice recognized. In the face of "official memory" those who are marginalized must struggle to hold on to their own representations, and can flounder when there are no social mirrors that accurately and meaningfully reflect their experiences. A myopic focus on the present through the haze of a fixed and glorified past also means that the broader society is bereft of the kind of deep historical knowing that could make genuine progress on racial matters possible.

Because history persists into the present and shapes the future, memory is an important site for social struggle. The culture wars over what and how history is to be taught illustrate well the powerful stakes invested in controlling official memory (Symcox, 2002). As a bridge between past and present, social memory shapes identity, informs our interpretations of events, fuels grievances and claims on the present, and suggests what we might imagine for the future. Through the practice of uncovering concealed stories we work against the grain to resurrect hidden histories/social memories, learn from the "confiscated heritage" of subjugated peoples and expose the constructed nature of official representations of reality.

Concealed stories that counter mainstream accounts of racial reality can be powerful educational tools. Such stories "are full of dangerous, subversive revelations that undermine the whole fabric of inequality" (Levins Morales, 1998, p. 18) and thus provide critical intelligence so necessary for antiracist work. They help us affirm and learn from the experiences of those whose stories have been marginalized as we seek more inclusive and varied ways to live and develop individual and social potential. They can help people in the dominant group develop a different kind of listening in which we seek out rather than avoid stories that challenge our assumptions about the world and begin to understand the ways we are implicated in the lives of others (Boler, 1999; Walsh, 2007). Concealed stories enable people from all racial groups to develop more critical awareness about how racism operates so as to more consciously challenge its grip on our relationships and social structures.

Exploring the Genealogy of Racism through Concealed Stories

Concealed stories are literally everywhere, "hidden in plain view" (Loewen, 2006), usually familiar within communities of color that preserve and pass them on, but mostly invisible or overlooked in the mainstream. Sometimes they may be suppressed, consciously or unconsciously, to avoid traumatic and painful memories of dehumanization by those on the receiving end of racism, or to evade the guilt and moral responsibility of those who benefit from a stratified racial system, but they are there to be recovered.

Central to the Storytelling Project Model is our belief that a properly supportive counter-storytelling community must be intentionally created to bear witness to and support "the naming of trauma and the grief, rage and defiance that follow" (Levins Morales, 1998, p. 16). Within an intentional storytelling community, people from different racial locations relate their own and hear other's stories, working together to make the connections that are hidden by dominant narratives about racial life. Using written and performance exercises, interviews, dialogues and discussions with people from one's own racial group and with others from across racial groups, we evoke experiences with race and racism as a basis for revealing the patterns that connect.

The arts provide a compelling vehicle for memory work because they provoke our senses, activate our emotions, spark visceral contradictions and generate more embodied awareness of what we encounter in our social world. We call upon written and oral narratives and poetry, visual art and media, music and dance to draw out concealed stories about racial experience (Kirschke, 2007). We collect stories from multiple communities and contexts, and (re)present our own stories visually, musically and physically to generate new expressions of community and possibility. A wealth of sources are available for recovering concealed stories by shifting to the foreground that which is usually background to the stock stories that keep them hidden.

An Example of Memory Work

The following visualization and writing exercise, introduced by artist Roger Bonair-Agard to the Storytelling Project creative team, provides an example of memory work through the arts. The exercise draws on firsthand accounts of moments in which we are socialized about race. The stage is set by guiding the group through a progressive relaxation exercise to shut out external stimuli and focus internally. We are asked to imagine ourselves at earlier stages of our lives, starting with the present moment and moving backwards in five- or ten-year increments until reaching around five years of age. We are prompted to visualize in our mind's eye a vivid physical image of ourselves at that young age, sitting on the lap of or talking with someone we love—a parent or grandparent, beloved aunt or uncle, or other significant adult—and to imagine a conversation with that person about race. We might recall an actual conversation but we could also construct a conversation from what the person might have said. Playing out the conversation in our mind's eye, we note the affect, the words and language used, and the lessons, implicit and explicit, about race in this emerging "memory."

Once we have completed the visualization, we spend time, five minutes or so, writing about the scene we visualized, noting as much of the dialogue, affect and our own responses in the situation as we can recall. We then pair up with another person and read what we have written aloud as our partner bears witness to the frequently emotional, often painful responses it provokes. Once each person has read her/his story to the other, we analyze the stories together to consider what they tell us about how race is taught and learned, consciously and deliberately, as well as unconsciously and inadvertently, from those we love and trust.

When we come back together as a whole group we discuss specific examples from the stories and trace patterns across them. For example, participants of color often describe a person they love instilling advice for dealing with a hostile white world, responding to racial barriers they are sure to encounter, suppressing oneself in order to be safe, or maintaining dignity in the face of prejudice and discrimination.

Roger illustrates through reading a poem he wrote titled "Bullet Points" (excerpted here):

You are Black. Not Negro
Not Nigger
Not Brown. Not Mixed
Not you have some German on your mother's side
From your great-grandfather because no one can
See that anyway
You are Black . . .

White people cannot be trusted
Be cordial. Be polite
But white people must prove themselves
Before they can be trusted . . .

White participants occasionally relate memories of being deliberately taught racial animus by someone they love. More frequently, however, they describe overt and covert messages about maintaining "appropriate" social distance, learning to fear those who look or speak differently, or being taught to express tolerance toward those less fortunate —with the implication of superiority embedded in that position. After the exercise I write in my journal:

I think of my grandmother, someone I adored as a child. I imagine myself sitting on her lap. If she were to say something about race, what would she say? She might say, "You should be kind to all people. You should not call names." She might also say races shouldn't mix. We should be with our own people. She might even say we are more civilized, they are good people but they don't care about education like we do, telling me I must be smart and study hard and learn. All this she would say in a gentle way, in a way a five-year-old cannot refute. Racism with a kind face, imbibed on the lap of someone I love.

These "memory" stories can be emotionally wrenching for both tellers and listeners. A strong and supportive counter-storytelling community that is willing to face and not smooth over conflicting feelings of guilt, anger, pain, shock and despair helps us pay attention to and learn from the feelings and lessons these stories evoke.

As we link our individual stories into a collective story we discern patterns of racism. We see how dominance and subordination are engendered, even against our own desires. We witness how our stories are interconnected, how advantage and disadvantage are constructed. It becomes impossible for a white person to say, "I never owned slaves, so I'm not responsible for the aftermath." We come to know in our guts that we are responsible and must be responsive to what our collective history has wrought if we are ever to be truly free in the present. We experience at a visceral level how everyone, regardless of race, is dehumanized, albeit in racially specific ways, through socialization into a racialized system. Such deep recognition creates the conditions for engaging more consciously with difference, recognizing the individual and collective work necessary for developing commitments to challenge these patterns in our institutions and personal lives. Through exercises such as this we (re)discover concealed stories about how racial consciousness is shaped and transmitted from within families and communities, but linked to patterns in the larger society that transcend individual experience.

Retrieving Concealed Stories through Visual Art

Visual art is another powerful medium for juxtaposing contradictory stories, sparking alternative ways of seeing and engaging our critical faculties. For example, art educator and creative team member on the Storytelling Project, Dipti Desai illustrated the juxtaposition of stock and concealed stories by engaging the creative team in an analysis of images created by contemporary visual artists.[1] One image we examined together is "Wilderness" by artist David Avalos (Lippard, 1990). In this 1- by 8-foot panel Avalos has superimposed letters to spell the word "Wilderness" over a diverse array of photographs of Native American faces, men and women, from different Native communities and parts of the country. Above them, the artist has printed a definition of "wilderness" drawn from a standard dictionary: "a tract or region uncultivated or uninhabited by human beings." This provocative piece vividly juxtaposes the very real presence of Native people against the idea of pristine, uninhabited wilderness so popular in stock stories of discovery and westward expansion. We are invited to identify the stock story being contested in this image, to think about the concealed stories represented in the faces of the people and to consider the stock stories they challenge by their very presence.

Another example from contemporary art is "Mine/Yours" by artist Fred Wilson. In this piece, Wilson juxtaposes two side-by-side images: On the right is placed a collection of the stereotyped images of black dolls popular as collectors' items throughout the south. On the left is an actual photograph of an African American sharecropper family from post-slavery times, showing family relationships, children and elders, together. The caption "Mine/Yours" challenges the observer to look behind the stereotyped images (Yours) to the real people hidden by racist images (Mine) and recognize the human relations and experiences obscured by static stereotypes. Contemporary artists offer a wealth of visual images that question and challenge taken-for-granted assumptions about racial/social life that can be used in teaching about concealed stories (see for example, Atlas & Korza, 2005; Desai, 2000; Desai, Hamlin, & Mattson, 2009; Lippard, 1990).

Through images such as these, artists expose contradictions, unsettle assumptions and compel us as viewers to question and look anew. Contemporary art provides many such examples that can be used to engage people in thinking about dominant stories, to consider what they leave out or conceal, and to listen anew to concealed stories in ways that force us to question what dominant stories naturalize as true.

Juxtaposing Versions of History

When we juxtapose the stock stories in American history with concealed stories pulled forward by revisionist historians, we can trace the construction of white racial advantage over time. The elements of the historical stock story we learn in school are familiar to every school child. With rare exceptions, we learn to uncritically view the founding fathers as wise visionaries, and the Constitution as an ideal document. We typically do not learn about the race-based decisions to explicitly enshrine race, as well as class and gender, privilege in founding documents created by an all-white, male, land-owning group (Feagin, 2006). We generally study slavery as a dark, but singular, episode in our past. We do not learn that slavery or legal segregation have been in place for almost 90 percent of our history as a nation and that the vestiges of this history persist in patterns of racism today (Feagin, 2006). We learn little about the long history of government retreat in the face of white resistance to racial remedies or about ensuing government policies and practices that ensured black peonage and sustain white advantage into present times (Blackmon, 2008; Lipsitz, 2006; Oliver & Shapiro, 1997).

Even when we do acknowledge shameful episodes in the past, no connection is made between then and now. "We have no critical sense of the trajectory of our history with race and thus no grounding for understanding its persistent presence in our lives and institutions today" (Loewen, 2006, p. 473). The happy stock story taught to school children that Native Americans welcomed the Pilgrims (the Thanksgiving stock story) has in some cases been modified to acknowledge that vast numbers of Native people were killed and their land stolen by Whites. Yet the realities of the lives of Native American Indians today, even the fact of their contemporary existence, remain invisible, locked in stereotyped images of the past, with no exploration of ongoing white complicity and responsibility for their situation today (Churchill & Trask, 2005; Stannard, 1992; Wright, 2005).

Historical accounts by revisionist historians that tell this history and make these connections can be unearthed to help us understand present-day racial patterns. This is particularly helpful for uncovering how white racial advantage, presented as neutral and normative, is actually constructed. Posing as history detectives we begin to ask questions about what is taken as unquestioned truth but may tell only part of the story. For example, why is it that the population in certain parts of the country is all or predominantly white? Loewen (2006) explores the deliberate creation and maintenance of all-white towns ("sundown towns") throughout the country following Reconstruction, towns where black people, and in many areas Native Americans and Mexicans, were literally run out of town. We learn that it is not an accident that parts of the country are all or mostly white but in fact the result of deliberate expulsion and exclusion, contributing to the concentration of people of color in urban areas, often the only areas where it was historically safe for them to reside.

How did it come about that Whites own so much more of the wealth of this country than any other group? We typically highlight the merit and hard work of those who are successful, for example valorizing the gumption and struggles of settlers moving west. Yet revisionist scholarship has now revealed the ways that government policy rigged the system to the advantage of white people from earliest times. A few examples: slavery and the coerced free labor of black people created major advantages for white slaveholders and others who benefited from a plantation economy—some estimates put this in the trillions of dollars. The 1830 Indian Removal Act expelled the Cherokee from the east and gave their land to Whites. The Homestead Act of 1862 created a massive redistribution of Indian land to mostly white homesteaders and the Southern Homestead Act of 1866 meant to benefit black freedman (40 acres and a mule) had, because of ongoing racial discrimination, minor effects for black people but major effects for white landowners. White racial preferences in immigration laws from the 1790s through 1965 worked for the benefit of white immigrants. The 1935 Social Security Act excluded agricultural and domestic workers (where Blacks and Latinos were largely concentrated) while the 1935 Wagner Act enabled white workers to unionize for better wages and working conditions, while permitting the exclusion of non-whites.

> But it was another racialized New Deal program, the Federal Housing Administration, that helped generate much of the wealth that so many white families enjoy today. These revolutionary programs made it possible for millions of average white Americans—but not others—to own a home for the first time. The government set up a national neighborhood appraisal system, explicitly tying mortgage eligibility to race. Integrated communities were ipso facto deemed a financial risk and made ineligible for home loans, a policy known today as "redlining." Between 1934 and 1962, the federal government backed $120 billion of home loans. More than 98% went to whites. (Adelman, 2003)

These explicit government policies enabled the accumulation and intergenerational transfer of wealth to white people, and rendered these unavailable to Blacks and other people of color, thus creating the gross racial disparities in assets we see today (Feagin, 2001; Katznelson, 2005; Lipsitz, 2006; Oliver & Shapiro, 1997). A DVD produced by California Newsreel titled "Race: The Power of an Illusion" (Adelman, 2003), an excellent teaching tool, vividly recounts the story of the construction and perpetuation of white privilege.

Resurrecting and teaching this history not only provides a more accurate explanation of the roots of inequality today, and thus a better likelihood of their effective remedy, but makes history relevant and engaging to young people who are turned off in school. There is some evidence that youth of color are much less willing than white students to uncritically accept a valorized version of history that ignores the struggles and contributions of their communities (Epstein, 2009). Exposure within families and communities that preserve and pass on the history and struggle (concealed stories) of their people make them skeptical of the homogenized history (stock stories) taught in schools. While such skepticism could provide grounds for a more critical reading of history, without teachers who know the racialized history of our country and who have the ability to teach it critically, students of color often feel alienated from a curriculum in which they do not see themselves reflected (Epstein, 2009; Roberts, Bell & Murphy, 2008).

White students, as well, are prevented from coming to grips with the problems and limitations of a distorted history that ill prepares them for understanding systemic racism and living in equality with others. Seldom do they learn about the structured benefits of whiteness and its implications for their lives today, or about how they might draw on more accurate history to think about how they could work for justice as equals with others. Nor do they learn about role models of white people who have fought against racism throughout our history and whose example could guide them today (Aptheker, 1992; Brown, 2002; Derman-Sparks, Ramsey & Edwards, 2006; Zinn, 2003).

Below I describe some of the lessons we have used to teach about concealed stories. Tools for tracing concealed stories include analyzing the poetry, music and literature created by people from marginalized groups as well as systematically applying the lens of race (as well as class and gender) to look at history and social science data. We pose questions such as: "If people were truly equal in this society, what would we expect to see in terms of access, participation and achievement in our institutions? What does social science data tell us about the current status of different groups?" Using such questions to look at data can reveal racialized patterns in government policies, schooling, wages, incarceration rates and other arenas of social life that are invisible, taken as natural, or attributed to characteristics of the group rather than to systemic patterns of discrimination and exclusion. These data help us see concretely how race is constructed and reconstructed to advantage Whites as a group.

The Storytelling Project Curriculum engages students as detectives who search out historical records and statistics about how racial status affects housing, credit, income and asset accumulation, incarceration, schooling, life expectancy and access to health services using statistics available in government documents, textbooks and on the Web. They use tools of critical analysis to explore questions that are immediately relevant to their own circumstances and share their research with each other, often using art to represent their findings visually and physically.

Activity: Income Distribution, Race and Mobility

After exploring the American Dream, students want to know why, despite the struggles they witness in their families and communities to get ahead, they still so often fail. We turn to an interactive game (Yeskel & Wright, 2007) in which students physically represent income distribution in a way that makes economic policy and distribution of wealth concrete and accessible. In this activity, ten chairs, each representing 10 percent of the country's wealth, are placed in the front of the room and ten volunteers sit one in each chair. One volunteer represents the top 10 percent and since this group owns 60 percent of the country's wealth, five students are told to move over so that the student representing the top group can sprawl over six chairs, squeezing the other volunteers into the four remaining chairs.

Next the facilitator tells the group that the above percentages were actually for the year 1976. If we look at 2004 (or look up current figures) the top 10 percent owns 70 percent of the wealth, so seven volunteers must squeeze into three chairs. Students return to their seats and the group discusses what they experienced/observed. We note that the figures used above are based on class. We then ask students to think about what they think the percentages would look like if they were based on race. Students research this question and make charts where race and class are combined using contemporary statistics. They discuss who owns the wealth in the United States and question why it is this way. They consider what would have to change in order for merit to overcome race/class barriers to mobility.

Activity: Education and White Advantage

In a subsequent activity, students view the DVD "Echoes of Brown" (Fine et al., 2004) in which youth present data they have collected on segregation and white advantage in contemporary public schools. In this provocative and engaging video the data are presented through poetry, spoken word and performance. After viewing the DVD, students write their own stories or poems drawing on the data presented to describe educational inequities they experience in their own schools. In an extension of this activity, they work in pairs to write a Dick and Jane story, substituting Maria (a student of color) and Jane (a white student). In their stories they try to capture how these two characters move through the education system, noting at least four areas where white privilege/advantage is operating and the effects on their characters. They share their stories and discuss the outcomes of cumulative white advantage over time, exploring how their characters' lives might look as they move into adulthood and the future. This activity begins to lay bare how access to the American Dream is mediated and the impact for excluded groups.

Activity: The American Dream—Who Is Left Out?

In this activity we turn to concealed stories related by poets and artists of color that challenge the American Dream and look beneath its shiny façade to reveal the lives of people in the margins. This lesson looks at the stories of those who, despite perseverance and hard work, do not realize the American Dream. Students work in groups to analyze and prepare a dramatic reading of the poem "Puerto Rican Obituary" by Pedro Pietri (Pietri, 1973). This eloquent and moving poem describes the dedication to the American Dream of those who are so often excluded. Groups perform readings of the poem and then discuss the concealed stories the poem reveals, considering whether and how these stories are told in mainstream media and how they contradict stock story images and stereotypes of Puerto Ricans, Latinos and other people of color.

Students also read "A World Without Black People" by Philip Emeagwali (info@pemeagwali.com), a story that takes a young boy through daily activities where inventions by black people are not available. For example, he is not able to find shoes, iron his clothes, comb or brush his hair, use a dustpan or mop, etc.—all activities that require an implement invented by a black person. Students discuss their reactions to this story and consider why we don't typically learn information about important inventions African Americans and other people of color have made.

Students then write their own story, skit or play imagining a day in New York City without people of color. What work would not get accomplished? What would happen to the city? What losses might occur, services not be available, etc.? They perform their skits/plays for each other and discuss what this illustrates about who contributes to the American Dream, whose contributions are recognized and whose omitted, and begin to consider how this might be changed. As follow up, students are encouraged to research information about Native Americans, Asian Americans, Latinos and African Americans that are often concealed in mainstream media, textbooks and popular discourse.

Activity: Criminalization of Youth of Color

This activity engages students in a deeper look at the way problems are framed in schools with a high population of minority students, schools that are often over-policed and under-funded. They read a city hall press release on increasing policing in targeted schools juxtaposed with a NYCLU (New York Civil Liberties Union) report telling stories of individual students caught up in the new policing regime (see Storytelling Project Curriculum for references). Students discuss how the problem is defined in the city hall report, who is involved in thinking about the problem, consider solutions to it, and discuss how they feel reading these reports.

Next, students create a "Role on the Wall." In groups, students are assigned a "character" such as teacher, principal, student, NYPD security guard, parent. Centered on their newsprint they draw a large outline of a body. Outside the body they write words and phrases that convey what other people say about this "character" and what this character is expected/pressured to do by the outside world. On the inside of the body, students write words or phrases that convey their character's hopes, desires and fears. Groups hang their pictures on the wall around the room, do a gallery walk to look at each body's associated words/ images. What are the similarities among the characters in terms of needs, fears, hopes, etc.? What are the differences? What would have to happen for the characters to exist harmoniously in the school?

As students consider the concealed stories that shape experiences with race and racism, uncovering concealed stories from history, social science data, poetry and their own experiences, they gain tools for critiquing stock stories about the American Dream, mobility, meritocracy and access as these are portrayed in the media and mainstream discourse. They begin to see that the stock story can be contradicted and challenged and that they have tools for uncovering information they need in order to develop an informed critique of the status quo as a basis for thinking about actions they might take to change things.

Conclusion

Through contrasting stock and concealed stories, we use the information in concealed stories to unpack and critically analyze the polished stock stories at the center of American life and trace their connections to larger patterns of discrimination and exclusion in our culture. The juxtaposition of stock and concealed stories provides a vantage point for seeing differently, unsettling the presumptive truth in stock stories and showing them to be as partial and incomplete as any other story—thus open for contestation.

In contrasting stock and concealed stories, we can work the juxtapositions backward or forward. We can start with stock stories and then look for the concealed stories underlying them. Or we can begin with concealed stories, analyzing what they reveal about stock stories that we take for granted. Once we have exposed the stock stories and unearthed the concealed stories that show the self-interested protection of advantage, we can turn to resistance stories. How have people fought against the stock stories in the past? What can we learn from resistance stories to inform antiracist practice today? This is the topic of the next chapter on resistance stories.

4

RESISTANCE STORIES

Drawing on Antiracism Legacies and Contemporary Examples to Map the Future

In the poetics of struggle and lived experience, in the utterances of ordinary folk, in the cultural products of social movements, in the reflections of activists, we discover the many different cognitive maps of the future, of the world not yet born.

(Kelley, 1996, p. 10)

Resistance stories are the third story type in the Storytelling Project Model. These are stories that narrate the persistent and ingenious ways people, both ordinary and famous, resist racism and challenge the stock stories that support it in order to fight for more equal and inclusive social arrangements. They draw from a cultural/historical repository of narratives by and about people and groups who have challenged racism and injustice; stories that we can learn from and build on to challenge stock stories that we encounter today.

Resistance stories come from several sources. Some resistance stories emerge from (formerly) concealed stories that reveal the small and large ways people before us have challenged racism in their communities and personal lives as these are documented in writing and passed down orally. Other kinds of resistance stories come from the work of contemporary artists, educators and activists who model ways to challenge racism through their artwork, pedagogy and political actions. By illustrating antiracist perspectives and practices, resistance stories expand our vision of what is possible and form the foundation for ongoing creation of new stories that can inspire and direct antiracism work in the present.

Dictionary definitions of resistance use terms such as "confrontation," "opposition," "struggle" and "conflict." These terms typically have a negative connotation, especially when applied to those who challenge the status quo. In the Storytelling Project Model, we ascribe positive interpretations to these terms. Resistance—as in the ability of an organism to ward off what is damaging—is healthy. Just so, resistance to racism, and other forms of oppression, is healthy for our body politic. It makes a society stronger, more resilient and democratic, and more effective at fostering the well-being of its people. Likewise, confrontation, opposition and struggle connote for us proactive engagement with issues of racism so necessary to generate change. In our view, conflict is inevitable when antiracist ideas and principles clash with a status quo that passively allows racism to continue. Such conflict can be dynamic—it catalyzes a sense of being morally alive, actively engaged and willing to struggle with others toward a better world.

Resistance stories, as a heritage of collective struggle to which we can lay claim in the present, are too seldom taught (often remaining as concealed stories that need to be unearthed and reclaimed). Yet they have the potential to inspire and mobilize people to see themselves as proactive agents and participants in democratic life. Such stories have the capacity to instruct and educate, arouse participation and collective energy, insert into the public arena and validate the experiences and goals of people who have been marginalized, and model skills and strategies for effectively confronting racism and other forms of inequality.

Even when such narratives are raised though, they too often focus on iconic stories about heroic individuals; stories that obscure and sanitize the collective struggles that drive social change, and thus fail to pass on necessary lessons about how such change actually comes about. The Rosa Parks story is one example. In the typical mainstream story, Parks is most often presented as a woman who one day was simply too tired to stand and courageously refused to move to the back of the bus. The full story of Rosa Parks and the Montgomery bus boycott, however, is one of careful and organized planning over time by a group of people committed to challenging segregation (Collier-Thomas & Franklin, 2001; Kohl, 2004). The authentic story of Rosa Parks provides valuable information about how organized resistance comes about, filling in gaps and providing lessons, guidance and models for organizing opposition to racism and other forms of oppression.

As counter-stories to the status quo, resistance stories (like concealed stories) challenge stock stories that reinforce power relations by bending resistance to suit their own ends. For example, resistance when framed in opposition to British domination in the Revolutionary War serves as a foundational story about the American spirit of independence and drive for freedom, a story that is preserved and passed on in textbooks, movies and public rituals. Yet, Native American resistance to domination by those same colonists is characterized as savage, hostile, and legitimately to be subjugated. When people of color resist the oppressive authority of the dominant white racial group, resistance is often characterized as negative, angry, inappropriate, something requiring suppression and subjugation. The lessons of resistance in our history as a nation are plentiful but too often hidden under the crust of official stock stories that serve the interests of the status quo. Yet, resistance stories are there to be resurrected and used to inspire people today, and indeed offer ways to make history relevant and meaningful to the present (Green, 2000; Harding, 1990; Kelley & Lewis, 2000; Vickery, 2008; Zinn, 2003).

Youth Resistance and Educating for Democracy

More often than not, resistance has an especially negative connotation when applied to marginalized youth living in inner city communities and attending under-resourced schools. Stock stories in media and popular culture stereotype them as defiant, in need of control, as oppositional only in negative ways, contributing to a deficit discourse that distorts their lives and ignores or minimizes the institutional barriers they face. They are racially coded in politics, media, and mainstream narratives as "at risk" or worse, as dangerous threats to society (HoSang, 2006). Indeed, the Reagan administration redefined young men of color as "super-predators" justifying harsher treatment by police and the courts through policies that continued under both Democratic and Republican administrations (Wilson, 2005). Contemporary youth are under constant surveillance on the streets and in their schools, subjected to curricular, disciplinary and monitoring systems designed to contain, rather than educate and lovingly guide them (Noguera, 2008). "Rather than being cherished as a symbol of the future, youth are now seen as a threat to be feared and a problem to be contained...Youth are currently being framed as both a generation of suspects and a threat to public life" (Giroux, 2004, p. 85).

The political, social and economic conditions facing young people today are further exacerbated by neo-liberal policies and demographic changes that severely limit opportunities for good schooling, decent jobs, affordable health care, and self-fulfillment (Foundation, 2009; Fulbright-Anderson et al., 2005; Giroux, 2003; Isaacs, 2007; Lipman, 2003; Sleeter, 2008). Welfare "reform" and economic recession place a greater burden on young people who have to take on more family responsibilities, and some studies indicate that today's youth are the first generation in a century that is not likely to be better off than their parents. "Compared to previous generations, today's 20 and 30-somethings earn less, carry more debt and pay more for everything from health care to housing. The current recession has only exacerbated these conditions, hitting young people of color and those without a college degree the hardest" (Draut, 2008, p. 38).

The needs and concerns of a younger generation that is browner and poorer are often ignored or downplayed by a whiter and wealthier older generation that controls mainstream media and policy institutions. Neo-conservative pundits argue that funding good schools, qualified teachers and smaller classrooms is "throwing away money" while claiming that deploying resources toward privatization of schooling and high stakes testing is "accountable."

This framing is used to justify the increasing "rationing of curriculum" (Darling-Hammond, 1995), widespread use of standardized testing and test-driven/test-prep materials (Sleeter, 2007) and zero-tolerance policies of high security, uniformed police, and metal detectors that seek to control, rather than educate young people in urban schools (Anyon, 1997; Giroux, 2003; Noguera, 2003; Wacquant, 2009). Such policies locate the source of problems in students and their communities rather than in the persistent and pernicious racial and class patterns that circumscribe their lives. This view of young people effaces their rights as citizens and their potential to be vitally engaged in challenging and shaping institutions and practices that govern their lives.

These circumstances also proscribe and limit white youth who question the status quo, challenge racism and white privilege, and demand changes in their schools, families and communities. As young people they are expected to conform to roles dictated by others and if they step out of line too far, they are quickly reminded of their "place" (see for example, Love & Phillips, 2007). Indeed, as Ginwright and Cammarota (2006, p. xv) note, "in many ways youth from working poor communities are second class citizens—as with Jim Crow segregation, they are subjected to hostile laws and unfair policies but have no rights to change them."

Resistance for Liberation Rather than Survival

Theories of resistance play a prominent role in research and writing about youth. Initially, oppositional practices by youth who are disenchanted with school were analyzed as self-defeating and ultimately reinforcing of the status quo (see for example, Fine, 1991; Willis, 1981). Later, the constructive potential of resistance as a force in young people's lives received more attention. Ward (1996), for example, employs the concepts of "resistance for liberation" versus "resistance for survival" to contrast the positive and negative potential in resistance. In her work with African American girls, Ward distinguishes between behaviors that are self-defeating or self-destructive, quick fixes or short-term solutions that are ultimately adaptations to racism (resistance for survival), with behaviors that strengthen girls in the face of oppressive and dehumanizing social patterns (resistance for liberation). Ward writes that resistance for liberation should prepare young people "to resist their racial subordination by learning how to identify racism and knowing when, where and how to develop the strategies they will need to withstand and overcome the unpredictability of today's manifestations of racial oppression" (Ward, 2000, p. 40).

In a similar vein, some critical race theorists use the term "resilient resistance" to describe strategies students develop to survive and succeed within structures of domination while others use "transformational resistance" to connote behavior that is "not reactionary, conformist or self-defeating but rather political, collective, conscious, and motivated by a sense that individual and social change is possible" (Solorzano & Delgado-Bernal, 2001, p. 318). Several writers draw on Vine Deloria's term "survivance" to illustrate a combination of survival and resistance, adaptation and strategic accommodation that people develop to both survive and contribute positively to their communities (Brayboy, 2005a; Grande, 2004). "Resistance for liberation," "resilient resistance," "transformational resistance" and "survivance" are all terms that capture the positive and empowering potential in youth practices of resistance; practices that are essential to their engagement as agents who can "act effectively in their own behalf and against institutional and systemic patterns and practices that marginalize them" (Solorzano & Delgado-Bernal, 2001, p. 319).

In the Storytelling Project we understand youth resistance as just such a positive and constructive force. We recognize youth as actors with capacity to uncover problems in their schools and communities and utilize their energy, perspectives and experience as resources for educational and social change. A primary goal of the Storytelling Project Curriculum is to foster spaces in classrooms (counter-story-telling communities) where young people can engage as social critics, develop a historical understanding and strong critique of racism and other forms of oppression (Adams, Bell & Griffin, 2007) and generate effective ways to challenge oppressive conditions in their schools and communities. The curriculum situates the lived experiences of students, particularly young people of color, at the center. Lessons are designed to draw upon their (concealed) stories as the ground for critically examining stock stories about racism and other social issues that impact their lives. We introduce resistance stories to study oppositional strategies and tactics that can inspire and support emerging/ transforming stories about changes they wish to bring about in their schools and communities.

A counter-storytelling community that validates the stories young people bring to the classroom can create "pockets of hope" (de los Reyes & Gozemba, 2002; Morrell & Duncan-Andrade, 2008) where they build a community of resistance drawn from their shared history of being "other" (Brayboy, 2005b; El-Haj, 2009). Their stories become the basis for analyzing and challenging racism and other forms of injustice they encounter in their lives. From this stance they learn to productively use their marginality (hooks, 1990) to create possibilities for change. Through focusing on counter-stories of resistance, students engage in "the practice of freedom" (Freire & Freire, 1994; hooks, 1994), and take an active stance against the social barriers they face and toward new, more liberatory possibilities. In this way, the classroom becomes a supportive space for the exploration and expression of resistance and the development of emerging/transforming stories in which young people imagine alternatives to the status quo and develop proactive means to enact their vision.

Finding Resistance Stories in the Concerns of High School Youth

Stories that show the ways everyday people work together to resist injustice are a powerful tool for encouraging young people to consider their own role as actors and citizens in the public arena. Indeed, high school students who participated in the Storytelling Project Curriculum frequently expressed a yearning to know more about what they called "the smaller people" in history. While schools too rarely create communities where youth critique is invited, we cultivated a counter-storytelling community in two high school classrooms in the Bronx where stories by young people were welcomed and centered as the focus for learning (see Roberts, Bell & Murphy, 2008). Working with two amazing teachers of color, who in part shared and understood their students' experiences and were comfortable openly discussing issues of race and racism, we co-created with students a space of trust, honesty, and critical learning where they could actively fashion the curriculum to fit their interests and concerns.

Through dialogue students unearthed the contradictions of living daily with the consequences of racism in a society that claims race no longer matters. Students commented that teachers rarely want to talk about racism so simply putting race on the table was a novel experience. As one of the participating teachers noted: *"I think that most of them don't understand why it's not talked about, and they don't know how to deal with it...I think it's because people always say, 'Color doesn't mean anything' or 'I treat everyone the same.'"*[1]

Within a supportive counter-storytelling community, students enthusiastically engaged in analyzing stock stories, bringing in their own concealed stories about racial experience as contrast. In so doing, they surfaced "generative themes" that we could explore through the curriculum. For example, students' own experiences completely contradicted color-blind rhetoric they hear in school and in the mainstream media. They described how they are perceived and reacted to in a range of situations: riding on the bus, venturing into downtown Manhattan, participating in a debate judged by white professionals who stereotyped their Bronx accents and gave them a lower score.

> *They don't understand you because of the accent...[x] did an opening statement...She had good pace, but because she had good grammar, it didn't sound like her! How do you want us to speak? I think that they were assuming that because we are from the Bronx that we don't speak right.*

Students frequently expressed dissatisfaction with a curriculum that superficially focuses on stock stories about slavery and iconic figures from the Civil Rights era, but does little to help them reflect on concealed stories in their lives and their communities or learn about resistance stories that might support their capacity to imagine and generate alternatives specific to the historical moment in which they find themselves. For example, one student articulated a desire for historical information about the actions of ordinary people like themselves: *"We need to know more than just Martin Luther King and Malcolm X...they [teach] the most important people but the smaller people they do stuff too..."* As the "smaller" people, youth want to understand how racism operates and learn how they might challenge it effectively, but feel they get little guidance from social studies curriculum that seems frozen in time, or from adults who offer little current information or vision to guide them.

Another theme youth brought to the table centered on a sense that they were being pushed out of their neighborhoods. As students examined the concealed stories in social science data about how race sorts opportunity and access, one raised the issue of gentrification, a term he did not yet know but whose examples were quite clear to him: *"They trying to move everybody from Harlem... they trying to run everybody out... they trying to bring everybody to the Bronx because they want to keep Manhattan... the whole thing, Harlem too."* Their teacher validated this concern: *"A lot of students used to live in Washington Heights. They have left. They can't afford it anymore, and they see that everything's changing. They're saying, 'They're only raising rent because they know we can't afford it, so they're trying to get rid of us.' That's their understanding."* Students and teachers alike noted how race (and class) operate through gentrification and displacement of people of color in their communities and struggled together to make visible that which color-blind discourse conceals.

Students are hungry for spaces and curricula that provide context and historical knowledge to help them ground their own experiences and analyses. Linking the Storytelling Project Model to their felt concerns, they created sites within their schools for addressing critical social issues such as racism. As one teacher argued: *"They have such valuable opinions and beliefs and I think one of the reasons why our students don't get a lot of the information that comes out of the mainstream curriculum is that they don't care... they feel like it has nothing to do with them."*

Teaching/Learning through Resistance Stories

Within the counter-storytelling community they created, students began to value their already developing analyses of the social world, better understand the systems they contend with on a daily basis and approach course content with the conviction that their experiences could be an integral part of the curriculum. Below I illustrate how lessons from the curriculum utilized and built on some of the generative themes students raised for consideration.

Activity: Complete the Image

We introduced resistance stories through an activity called "Complete the Image" drawn from Boal's "Theatre of the Oppressed" (Boal, 2001, 2002; Schutzman & Cohen-Cruz, 1994) and developed by Kayhan Irani, an artist on the creative team with expertise and experience using these processes. Our purpose was to complicate and extend ways to look at resistance, since young people as much as adults are constrained by narrow popular views that stereotype resistance as negative. This activity helps students explore multiple forms of resistance, understand the variety and complexity of resistance strategies and problematize notions that resistance is necessarily ill mannered, aggressive, or violent.

In this activity, two volunteers come to the front of the classroom, face each other, shake hands and freeze. The facilitator draws an imaginary frame around the image they have created and asks the rest of the class as observers to speculate about its possible meanings. For example, the image could be two strangers meeting for the first time, friends greeting each other in a familiar way, a boss interviewing a candidate, competitors shaking hands before a match, etc. Students call out possibilities and then discuss how changing stances affect interpretations of the image. A few warm-up rounds demonstrate how the game is played and help students to limber up their observations and think creatively and playfully. The facilitator then asks the class to think of the term "resistance" and to complete images of resistance as one person at a time steps inside the frame and places themselves in the image. Observers analyze possible meanings each time the image changes and new participants step in and out over several rounds. Students consider what forms of resistance are enacted, listing these on the board for later discussion. As a culminating round, they create a whole group of resistance, gradually adding as many as want to join in.

The discussion following the game is key. Students use their observations of the game to discuss how changes were made and with what effect. They step back to consider the types of resistance observed—violent or nonviolent, outward or internal—and draw upon experiences from their own lives to illustrate. They note, for example, the many ways students can passively or actively resist in school—deliberately slowing down the pace of a lesson, talking or disrupting just to the edge of the rules, taking a long time to sharpen a pencil, using multiple bathroom breaks, daydreaming, etc. They discuss the purpose of resistance (avoid boring lessons or challenging assignments, cover up fear of failure, get notice or respect from other students, etc.). They consider the pros and cons of different strategies and assess the most effective ways to use resistance to meet their goals in different situations—for example, openly expressing boredom with tedious lessons and articulating their preference for learning that is relevant to their own concerns vs. passive resistance that may not change the situation; resisting disciplinary codes that are top-down and punitive by insisting on developing rules that respect their capacities and rights as school citizens rather than flaunting rules that bring punishment.

The level of discussion following games such as these is usually quite thoughtful and insightful. Students think deeply about what they observe in the game and make meaningful connections to real life. Through their shared analysis they develop a more explicit and nuanced understanding of resistance, think more critically about approaches to resistance and imagine alternatives for resisting consciously and proactively to reach their goals.

Activity: Still I Rise

In several activities students analyze poetry, literature and history to look at how resistance is expressed and to generate ideas. For example, a discussion of Maya Angelou's poem "Still I Rise"[2] (Angelou, 1978) elicits a discussion of internal forms of resistance—through creative self-expression, internal dialogues and fictional characters that show how seemingly individual, personal stories also can illustrate how an entire group of people resists oppression (see for example, Ward, 2000). Students read the Angelou poem silently and then in unison. They discuss questions such as: How does the author describe history? How does she distinguish between different types of history? What is truth as expressed in the poem? What is the poet resisting against? How? What does it mean to rise?

Students pair up to discuss their thoughts and consider the question: Where in your own experience do you see others or yourself "rising up" to racism (or sexism, classism, etc.)? How do you see yourself rising in your own life? Which forms of resistance identified in the game might you draw upon? For further reflection, students write their own poem about rising, using five pairs of couplets as in the Angelou poem. (See Christensen, 2000, 2009, and Cowhey, 2006, for other ideas and activities that can be used to look at resistance.)

Activity: Paint Down the Wall

In another activity students examine how artists use murals as a medium for representing issues they identify as important and express resistance to injustice. They read an essay on mural painting in Los Angeles originated by artist David Siqueiros in 1932 to affirm the history and indigenous roots of Mexican people (see Judy Baca, "The Birth of a Movement" at www.sparcmurals.org/usmx/birth/birth.html). Baca traces how muralists in Los Angeles have used this art form through the years to represent and discuss issues facing their communities that are ignored in the public sphere. She shows how the mural form, originated by Mexican muralists, has been adopted by other communities and groups—African American, Thai, Chinese, Jewish and women—to address their own concerns. The essay culminates in a description of "The Great Wall of Los Angeles," as an organizing tool to connect the diverse communities who live in L.A. through a joint mural project.

Students discuss the essay and relate it to their own situations. They discuss how black and Latino students, as well as U.S. born and immigrant students, are often pitted against each other in their schools and neighborhoods. They draw on a lesson from the curriculum to explore these concerns and consider how immigration policies relate to the development of racism and white privilege in the United States. They examine the murals created by SPARC: Social and Public Art Resource Center, to respond to anti-immigrant fervor (described in Baca's "The Birth of a Movement"). In groups of four to five they research particular immigration policies in history (using a time line adapted from Bell, Joshi & Zuniga, 2007) and then create their own murals in response. They discuss the symbols they have used in relation to different immigration policies and how the murals reflect resistance to racialized images and stereotypes of immigrants from various groups. In so doing, they develop knowledge about the history of immigration and racism in the United States and discover new ways to represent their ideas, knowledge and concerns through art.

Activity: Local Community Resisters

Looking at local history and examples, students next explore resistance to racism and other forms of injustice through studying role models in their own communities. They learn about Mothers on the Move (MOM), an activist organization in the South Bronx started more than ten years ago by mothers struggling for educational justice for their children. They read interviews from an essay about an oral history project of MOM (available at http://www.ashp.cuny.edu/mom/youth.htm). This essay generates ideas for how they might conduct interviews with people and organizations in their own communities. Imagining themselves in the role of investigative journalists planning to write a story about everyday resisters against racism (or gentrification, or other issues of concern) in their community, they design protocols and rehearse interviewing skills with each other. Based on what they learn from interviews they can then write articles for a local community paper, take photos, and/or compile a class newspaper to distribute in the community.

Through these and other activities, youth develop a much deeper understanding of resistance and see the possibilities for making their own claims on school knowledge, bringing their issues and concerns into the classroom and developing the kind of critical literacy that supports their proactive participation in addressing problems they see in their schools and neighborhoods. Not incidentally, they also develop skills and knowledge valued by traditional schooling (literacy and numeracy, historical knowledge, written and oral communication skills, cooperative endeavor, civic engagement), but through practices grounded in their concerns and interests. (For other examples see, El-Haj, 2007; Fisher, 2007; Morrell & Duncan-Andrade, 2008).

Conclusion

Learning about resistance and identifying examples of resisters in their own communities, prepares students to create emerging/transforming counter-stories that address issues they face in their own schools and neighborhoods. The prior examination of concealed and resistance stories grounds them in a broader historical and social context and helps them see that the problems they face are not idiosyncratic or individual but part of larger patterns; and that they are not alone but linked to a broader community (historical and contemporary) that has engaged with similar problems before them and can offer ideas that they can build on in the present. The exploration of resistance stories leads to emerging/transforming stories, the next and final story type in the model.

EMERGING/TRANSFORMING STORIES
Challenging Racism in Everyday Life

Make up a story. Narrative is radical, creating us at the very moment it is being created.

(Toni Morrison, 1993 Nobel Lecture)

Emerging/transforming stories are the fourth story type in the Storytelling Project Model. These are new stories we construct to challenge stock stories, build on and amplify concealed and resistance stories and take up the mantle of antiracism and social justice work through generating new stories to catalyze contemporary action against racism. Such stories enact continuing critique and resistance to stock stories, subvert taken for granted racial patterns and enable imagination of new possibilities for inclusive human community. Building on concealed and resistance stories, we envision alternatives to the status quo and generate strategies to realize our visions for racial equality in classrooms, schools and communities. Emerging/transforming stories arise from such questions as: What kinds of communities based on justice can we imagine and then work to make real? What kinds of stories can support our ability to speak out and act where instances of racism occur?

The term *emerging* connotes both the developing, embryonic nature of new stories and the historical and analytical roots that prepare the ground for their manifestation. Emerging, as in something newly or recently independent, also reflects our hope that the preceding story types have paved the way for developing the necessary critical knowledge, agency and self-determination to construct stories that counter the colonizing stock stories of the status quo. The term *transforming* describes the conversion of one form of energy into another to catalyze change. Combining these two terms—*emerging/transform-ing*—underscores that such stories arise from thoughtful analysis and careful study of history and culture, in contrast to ahistorical, indi-vidualistic stories that ignore the roots of racism and its systematic continuation into the present. Emerging/transforming also signifies the conversion of passivity into energetic force and the capacity to act in alignment with one's dreams toward a better future. These stories are always in the process of becoming as each generation or social group builds on and adds to common struggles for social justice.

A caution: In the diagram of the Storytelling Project Model (see Fig-ure 1.1), emerging/transforming stories point toward action/change as well as back toward stock stories, cautioning us to be aware of their capacity to transform as well as calcify. This reminds us of the need to continually stay vigilant for new manifestations of racism and other forms of injustice, and for concealed and resistance stories we have not yet considered. We realize this necessity, for example, in the evolution of understanding racism as we take up and learn from different groups whose stories may not initially have been considered in the analysis. Looking at racism (and other forms of oppression) from the perspec-tive of Native Americans or Latinos or Asian Americans or women or LGBT (lesbian, gay, bisexual and transgender) people raises different, previously unnamed or invisible, issues to consider. Thus the model highlights the contingent and evolving nature of our understanding of oppression and the need to work in coalition with others to develop the kind of "multi-perspectival" (Romney, 2005) understanding and awareness required to unearth and challenge entrenched patterns that reproduce racism in new forms.

In this chapter, I focus on the emerging/transforming stories of young teachers who desire to be social justice educators and work with their students to enact more democratic and inclusive educational practices inside their schools and outside in their communities. Such teachers can be advocates and allies for working with youth in the ways described in the preceding chapter. I argue that public schools, with all their problems, are an important site for struggle and demon-strate how I use the Storytelling Model in a seminar for pre-service teachers, returning to themes in earlier chapters to show how learn-ing about stock and concealed stories prepares them for imagining and enacting emerging/transforming stories in their curriculum and teaching.

Why Focus on Schools as Sites for Emerging/Transforming Stories?

Why focus on schools when we know the powerful role they play in reinforcing the status quo, reproducing race and class inequalities and other forms of injustice? Despite espousing principles of equality, democracy and opportunity, schools have historically failed to address the very real barriers to these ideals. "From colonial times to today, educators have preached equality of opportunity and good citizenship, while engaging in acts of religious intolerance, racial segregation, cultural genocide and discrimination against immigrants and nonwhites" (Spring, 2004, p. 3).

Despite this sordid history, schools are also sites where practices of intolerance and discrimination can be interrupted and the attitudes that support them changed. As long as we have a universal public education system, there is the, as yet to be realized, potential to create public spaces where people can encounter each other across social groups and together develop the skills, capacities and commitments needed to participate in the creation and maintenance of an inclusive democratic society (Comer, 2004; Fuhrman & Lazerson, 2005; Parker, 2003a, 2003b). Public schools hold out the possibility of becoming places where we live out multiracial democracy through grappling across our different locations with the patterns and practices that reinforce systemic racism and other forms of injustice (Banks, 2002; Parker, 2003a).

This potential is currently jeopardized by a national rhetoric that is evermore focused on standardized testing, accountability (in the narrowest, most utilitarian sense of the term), and individual advancement.

> Contemporary public education and reform are dominated by the goal of individual social mobility and status attainment, which justifies public schooling as a private good... The prevailing reform climate emphasizes students' scores on high stakes standardized tests as near-exclusive indicators of school success. The emphasis on students' market viability

contributes to reducing democracy to an economic concept—one that too often breeds selfishness, promotes a narrow conceptualization of social responsibilities of citizenship, and undermines a vision of community. (Fuhrman & Lazerson, 2005, pp. 132–133)

Reclaiming and working to enact the vision of public education as an incubator of democracy in our diverse society is urgent and compelling. Unfortunately, our teaching force is not currently prepared for this challenge. For one, the student population is more racially, ethnically, and linguistically diverse every day while the teaching population hovers at close to 90 percent white, middle class, female, and English monolingual (NCES, 2007; Villega & Lucas, 2002). This almost apartheid-like contrast between the teaching force and student bodies (Kailin, 1999) creates a serious barrier to the potential realization of democratic school spaces that can prepare a radically diverse student population to be agents and citizens of a multiracial democracy. Recruiting many more teachers of color, especially teachers who come from traditionally underserved communities, is critical to this project. Equally critical is making sure that the white/Anglo majority of current prospective teachers are knowledgeable about educational inequality and systemic racism. Teachers from all racial groups need to learn how to analyze, and challenge racism (as well as classism and other isms) as these affect school practices and procedures that differentially impact poor children, children of color, and children from diverse linguistic and cultural communities.

Teachers of color, while less likely than their white peers to deny the existence of racism or cling to naïve color-blindness, can benefit from an opportunity to discuss and analyze their own experiences with racism and learn antiracist strategies to address it in their schools and classrooms (L.A. Bell, 2003b). White teachers can gain from learning to identify and examine their own socialization, the unearned advantages of white racial dominance, and the conscious and tacit assumptions they hold about other racial groups and the social order (L. A. Bell, 2003b; Howard, 2006; Ladson-Billings, 2009; McIntyre, 1997; Marx, 2006). All teachers need to develop skills for detecting bias in classrooms and curriculum, analyzing and confronting racism in school patterns and practices, and helping students become future citizens prepared to enact fairness and justice in a multiracial democracy (Gordon, Della Piana & Keleher, 1998).

Using the Storytelling Project Model with Pre-Service Teachers

The Storytelling Project Model provides one way for teachers to explore both the overt and implicit assumptions they hold about race and racism and to develop strategies to teach knowledgably, conscientiously, and ethically in communities they often enter as privileged outsiders. The model asks aspiring teachers who are white and/or middle class to question beliefs that they occupy race and class neutral social positions. It exposes them to how racism operates in the broader society and in the schools they will enter as teachers, and gain historical and cultural knowledge to interrogate racism critically so as to teach toward a vision of racial justice.

For several semesters, I have used the Storytelling Project Model and story types to frame a seminar for undergraduate student teachers (L.A. Bell, 2010). I structure the syllabus, readings and course sessions using the four story types, beginning with an exploration of what it means to build a counter-storytelling community where race and racism can be productively explored in a racially diverse group. Seminar students use the story types as a set of lenses to examine and problematize their own socialization and the stock story assumptions they hold about student and community assets in the communities they enter as teachers, the sources of problems facing urban schools, their role as teachers, and the effects of racism on the institution of school. They also use the Storytelling Model and story types to think about and plan social-justice-oriented curriculum appropriate to their grade level/subject by using the story types implicitly to organize and plan curriculum, and/or explicitly teaching the story types directly to their students.

Problematizing Storytelling

In order to think about how to create counter-storytelling community in their own classrooms, we begin by reading authors who problematize storytelling and the roles of both listener and teller. For example, we read an article that contrasts storytelling in three different groups of learners (Sarris, 1990). In the first example, Sarris describes his reading of a Pomo Indian tale to a classroom of predominantly white, non-Indian students and notices how, semester after semester, what they remember and leave out of the story is shaped by the cultural lenses and experiences they bring as listeners. In the second scenario, Sarris describes a classroom of Native American students, where the issue is not understanding stories they all know and share but believing that their (concealed) stories matter in alien and alienating school contexts, and coming to believe that they can talk back (resistance stories) to the dominant story told in the mainstream curriculum. In a third example, Sarris discusses a diverse class of students of color who share no single, cultural story but through juxtaposing their varied stories, develop a shared understanding of and shape a collective response to a system that dominates them all (emerging/transforming stories). After discussing this essay, one of my students wrote about her realization that all stories are partial and political and that recognizing this can actually help her students develop as critical thinkers:

> *There is no space for a "neutral" story, as stories by their very nature are full of perspective and personal experience, which makes them all the richer as models for learning. Too often I feel that curricula attempt to erase their inescapable political foundations and biases, instead of using these explicitly to encourage students to critically analyze and grow as thinkers.*

The Sarris piece is powerful because it destabilizes notions of a universal perspective and helps student teachers see the power of racial positionality to shape perceptions, experiences and understanding of the world. We follow this with a close reading[1] of Toni Morrison's Nobel Prize acceptance speech (Morrison, 1993), in which she tells and retells a story from multiple perspectives, further opening up questions of positionality and power in stories we tell and further destabilizing notions of a single "true" or "correct" story.

In our seminar we also look critically at the notion of empathy and consider whether those who are outside of an experience, particularly within hierarchical relations, can step into the shoes of an "other" with any kind of validity. We read excerpts from *Feeling Power* (Boler, 1999) in which the author illustrates how patterns of thinking that deny power relations actually perpetuate injustice and reinforce self-interested positions passing as neutral. "Passive empathy," she argues, "produces no action toward justice but situates the powerful Western eye/I as the judging subject, never called upon to cast her gaze at her own reflection" (p. 159). Such empathy, she argues, leads to a "habituated numbness" that shields us from exposure and vulnerability that might lead to shared action to change the status quo. She notes, "These 'others' whose lives we imagine don't want empathy, they want justice... What is at stake is not only the ability to empathize with the very distant other, but to recognize oneself as implicated in the social forces that create the climate of obstacles that other must confront" (p. 166).

These readings provide a framework for thinking about racial positionality and our responsibility (response-ability) to systems of oppression and lead to an examination of stock stories of color-blindness. We read an essay from *Seeing a Color-Blind Future*, by critical race legal theorist Patricia Williams (1998) in which she explores the notion of color-blindness through a story about her black child's experience with his "color-blind" white teachers, whose uncritical embrace of color-blindness literally blinds them to the assaults he experiences on the playground at the hands of his white classmates. This essay is invariably revealing for students because it so clearly illustrates why assertions of color-blindness, especially by teachers, are so problematic. The response of a white student teacher illustrates the potency of these readings for prying open awareness about racial positionality and the dynamics of power and privilege:

> *The truth is that there is no such thing as an un-racialized situation.... The concealed story is that the color-blind mentality is detrimental to the goal of tolerance and equity... [T]o teach a child through your actions and words that their race doesn't matter is to belittle that child's very being, and the identity they have created for themselves up to this point. In addition, ignoring any influence of race prevents you as a teacher from identifying and challenging institutionalized racism.*

Course readings open up the possibility for talking about race and racism with the recognition that white people are also racially positioned and inescapably implicated in the systems they wish to interrogate. The readings lay the groundwork for discussing ways to create counter-storytelling community in which we are attentive to racial and other positionalities and strive to stay conscious of the hegemonic assumptions that often shape discourse. We develop guidelines both to construct our community in the seminar and to help students think about how they will create in their own classrooms the type of community where stretching beyond one's "comfort zone" (Griffin, 2007) to engage in counter-storytelling becomes possible. A student notes:

> *My learning edge is pushing myself to be comfortable with all these discussions that make me uncomfortable, so that I can continually reevaluate my own racialized position with respect to that of my students ... [I]f I'm comfortable, change can't happen.*

This discussion takes place just as student teachers are themselves entering a new elementary or high school placement, so creating community and a constructive classroom learning environment are very present in their minds. They become sensitized to noticing and looking at their own racial location, socialization, and experiences in relation to that of their students and begin to note ways that normative classroom discourse privileges and supports some students while overlooking and silencing others. They use the concepts of stock and concealed stories to consider whose stories and experiences are taken for granted and validated in curriculum and classroom practices and whose stories are hidden or ignored. This connection is made by a Korean American student teacher as she unearths and then compares her own early schooling experiences with that of a young girl in her classroom:

> *I ... remember that as a child I would yearn to see an Asian in my texts ... a longing to belong. In the classroom where I am student teaching, the majority of the texts have protagonists who are white ... On one of my first days [student teaching in 2nd grade], several girls asked if I was a sister to one of the Asian students in the class because, they said, "Your eyes look the same."*

The girl, herself, then proceeded to ask me if I was the same ethnicity as she and when I told her no [she was Chinese and I am Korean], she seemed dis-heartened. I felt she was looking to find something in me that is missing in the school ... This made me think about how important it is to be validated in the curriculum.

Having established norms for recognizing racial positionality and talking openly about race, we move to a discussion of stock and concealed stories about race, racism, teaching and learning in urban schools. Throughout the seminar, student teachers use the story types to examine their own racialized narratives and locations, and to listen and learn from the stories of their students, families, and communities in order to critique stock stories about color-blindness and meritocracy. Through reading, observations in schools, analysis of popular culture, and autobiographical reflection, we look at stock stories about working class and youth of color in urban schools and communities. We contrast stock stories about what they "need" evidenced in the grossly inadequate material and human resources dedicated to their education, compared to those provided to middle-class, white, suburban youth. One student teacher reflects on the power dynamics of language, cultural capital and agency.

Students who enter school speaking Spanish [as their first language], enter because succeeding in the United States demands a working knowledge of English (and often fluency). Attendance is all but obligatory. The students who enter school speaking English as their first language do so because they have made a decision to learn a second language. They have a choice. From the get go, the native Spanish speakers have no control over where they go, whereas the English-dominant students have agency and power in their world ... Working in a dual-language classroom in a country in which English is strongly reinforced as the "official" language, this message will always exist externally. All the more reason for what goes on in the classroom to be actively antiracist, anti-oppression, and pro-social justice.

As students read articles and books that portray the concealed stories, history and struggles of communities of color to achieve a decent education for their children (Michie, 1999; Perry, Steele & Hiliard, 2003; Valenzuela, 1999), they write about their own experiences of schooling and examine these alongside the readings and observations in their student teaching placements. For example, they read Theresa Perry's essay about the long history of struggle by black parents and communities against overwhelming odds to gain a decent education for their children (Perry, 2003). This concealed story is contrasted with the stock story, all too prevalent among teachers in urban schools, that defines the problem as parents who "don't care" about their kids' education.

This positioning of stock stories alongside concealed and resistance stories that challenge and talk back to them means that the "normative" story is up for question and analysis. White and middle-class students begin to see the racialized nature of their previously assumed neutral position.

> *I realized I had fallen into the stock story that I was not racist, that this was not my problem. I saw racism as something that I could help other people solve so they would not be discriminated against. I also hadn't understood until then how race (specifically) and privilege (generally) affected my relationships with people on individual levels, and the kind of difficult community building that is needed to lay these issues out on the table instead of only pretending they operated on some macro level, floating above our daily interactions.*

The juxtaposition of stock and concealed stories also creates a more welcoming space for students of color in the seminar to name, explore and recognize the validity of their racialized experiences and perspectives and be relieved of the pressure to go along with normative color-blind discourse.

> *I have experienced being educated in a wealthy school and being educated in a not so wealthy school. For a few years I was in a predominantly white elementary school and I remember being in a classroom with about twenty other students. All the teachers were white and the school had state of the art facilities but what I remember most was how I was isolated (along with the rest of the minorities). I remember knowing that I wasn't like the rest of the kids. During recess, most of the minorities would play together. Although I was getting a great education, I was not socially accepted.*

Students look at how stories about urban schooling are constructed to benefit some groups and disadvantage others and examine how such stories shape school policies, curriculum choices, grouping practices, relations with parents, and other issues. They develop the habit of interrogating normative practices by continually asking, "In whose interest does this particular story, practice, assumption operate? What concealed stories challenge or talk back to it?"

> *Once I had begun to think about how power and privilege operate on personal, individual levels and as part of larger systemic machinations, it became a constant lens for me to use in analyzing my classroom and myself. I worried about the ways that I might be setting expectations at different levels, how my teaching might be missing or connecting with certain students, what it meant for me to be a white teacher in a classroom of students of color teaching and learning about racism, how the curriculum was or was not built off of their experiences, cultures, and interests, and a host of other concerns. These thoughts and conversations helped me to develop an entire way of thinking and looking at the world beyond the classroom and pushed my commitment to social justice in all areas of my life.*

Creating Curriculum

Student teachers study resistance stories both to sharpen their own analytic skills and potential tools for teaching against the grain and to find curriculum materials they can use in their classrooms to introduce students to resistance stories. As their critique develops, student teachers search for alternative stories and examples to inspire and guide them in their struggle to teach in ways that work for the interests of their students and against an unjust status quo. They use the story types to design lessons and emphasize the value of teaching resistance stories to help young people become more critical thinkers who can be proactive in solving problems they name and analyze. One student teacher, after reading Kohl's essay on the Rosa Parks myth (Kohl, 2004), writes:

> *As an educator, it is important to show students this system so that they are aware of what they're up against but also so that they know they are not inherently at fault and can resist. Often what is left out is just as important as what is said. For example... much of what is left out from the Rosa Parks account speaks to the many levels in which [African American] culture is denigrated*

and history sugarcoated. The account leaves out details that could better encourage resistance to racism and also help to develop an empowering image of African Americans as resistors and activists within their community.

Building on resistance stories, student teachers then begin to generate emerging/transforming stories in which they imagine alternative images of what racial equality would look like in their classrooms and schools and then develop strategies to work toward the changes they envision.

I believe that "truth" stories [those that counter stock stories], whether they hear/see one from someone such as a teacher or peer or whether they experience them for themselves, give students a chance to see and share the change and justice we want for the world, as well as to practice being agents themselves. "Acting in solidarity with others is a learned habit," and being able to participate in monologues or role-playing gives students their own voices and empowers them to see and share alternatives to the oppression they and others experience.

Student teachers write a concluding story paper in which they review the four story types to frame what they have learned during the semester and outline plans for their continuing development as antiracist educators.

As I approach the end of my student teaching semester, I have come to realize that I have a voice and a story…Attending NYC public schools, it seemed to be that students of color were always left to fight for themselves and never had anyone truly fighting for them or with them…This experience gives me the courage to struggle for social justice and never give in to the stock stories about our students. A colleague said that [cooperating teacher] got too worked up over incidents that occur in the school and she should pick and choose her battles. What I came to understand was that it was all about the long-term battle; that she struggled to amplify her voice so that everyone could hear it. She taught me, "Always make sure someone listens."

Using the story types as a framework and/or as content, student teachers design curriculum units in their respective subjects that use the story types as a frame to help students generate emerging/transforming stories. For example, some student teachers design history units in which they introduce story types as analytic frames to help students read classroom texts critically. For example, students identify stock and concealed stories in history and search for historical evidence of resistance to racism, then use this information as a basis for considering conditions in their schools and communities, and ultimately to envision and act toward what they would like their schools and communities to become. A student preparing to teach high school science designs a chemistry unit that looks at DNA to debunk the notion of racial categories and to help her students understand the social construction of race. They use this knowledge to plan an assembly for the school where they talk about racial stereotypes and the dynamics that divide students along racial lines. Another student teacher creates a middle school literature unit using concealed and resistance stories to discuss racism in novels and poetry, drawing as well on contemporary youth hip-hop and spoken word. Students create their own spoken word poetry to comment on conditions they face as young people of color and perform their work at a community coffee shop.

> *Teaching resistance and counter-stories is much more than just asking higher order questions, though it is teaching students to examine and question their surroundings. It's not watering down what you teach to token holidays but rather addressing the realities of the world and all of the difficult issues in it, such as racism, sexism, poverty and violence and giving students the ability to actively make changes through social action projects. It's helping them realize that the society in which they live is not set in stone but rather shaped by the policies and people in it and that they have the power to effect change. Resistance and counter-stories can provide powerful examples of how this has happened in the past and serve as a model for what can be done now.*

Teachers make course content relevant and applicable to students' lives by actively teaching the skills of organizing, building coalitions, thinking about how to use power constructively and effectively to generate a compelling vision and mobilize action (see Storytelling Project Curriculum). The emerging/transforming stories students and their teachers generate catalyze a sense of possibility and help students develop confidence and the ability to act.

Conclusion

The Storytelling Project Model has proven to be effective at moving student teachers to consider the problems of color-blindness, understand racism, and develop a critical pedagogy for creating justice-focused curricular and classroom practices. Their ideas and examples are inspiring. Yet, how far they get in the development of their analysis is very much shaped by where they begin. Many students simply do not yet have enough knowledge or models to apply a consistent critique. Without further support and learning, expanding their knowledge and awareness of racism and its historical and contemporary operations, continuing to develop a critical stance will be difficult. The two student teachers quoted below illustrate that this is a life-long process requiring ongoing commitment and support.

> *I don't think that this will just happen one day, but rather will be a life-long process as a teacher. To be honest, it is very overwhelming to think of how much I don't know and how much I have to learn. However, reading about teachers who were able to effect change in their classrooms, I am inspired and motivated… because I see that it is possible.*

> *I have come to see learning to teach [for social justice] in the same light as learning a language. Even people who work diligently to master a language do not become fluent overnight. Or even over a week, or a month, or a year. Fluency is not a tangible internal snap, it is a gradual and time consuming realization that understanding a language requires intimacies and nuances that take a lifetime to generate.*

Although students are inspired in the context of the seminar, it is not possible in one semester to build the necessary awareness and knowledge to resist the constant recruitment back into the status quo that they will encounter in their lives and schools after graduation. Even students who are the most knowledgeable, activist, and committed and who have sustaining systems of support,[2] often encounter a school culture that makes it exceedingly difficult to enact antiracist curriculum and teaching practices. Yet, without teachers who have a vision of what socially just teaching can be, there is little hope that we can create the kinds of classrooms and schools where all children see themselves as central to the curriculum and agents of their own lives.

The Storytelling Project Model offers a compelling framework that new teachers, and others who work against racism, can use to actively critique the stock stories that reinforce inequality and racism, seek out concealed and resistance stories about the history, struggles, strengths, and aspirations of the diverse groups in our society, and use this knowledge to develop emerging/transforming stories that enact and sustain more inclusive and just educational and social practices. As a practical conceptual tool, it is our hope that the model is one that can be built on and added to over the long haul, operating as a caution against smug assumptions of all-knowing truth and as a reminder of what is possible when we listen to the multiple stories available for expanding our understanding as we work with others toward a multi-racial democratic vision.

6

CULTIVATING A COUNTER-STORYTELLING COMMUNITY

The Storytelling Model in Action

> We can negotiate a new understanding of democracy, but only if all of
> us are stakeholders in a common civic project...[W]hen the great wells
> of democracy are renewed and expanded to include those once outside
> America's social contract, a new history can begin.
>
> **(Marable, 2002, p. 328)**

The previous chapters have introduced the Storytelling Project Model
and defined and elaborated each of the four story types with examples to illustrate some of the diverse artistic, literary, historical and
pedagogical tools that may be used to examine each story type. In
this chapter we come full circle, back to the necessary first step of
creating counter-storytelling community—the essential foundation
for exploring stock and counter (concealed, resistance and emerging/
transforming) stories. In order to highlight counter-storytelling community building in practice, I use the extended example of a five-day,
intensive summer institute for teachers. I trace the evolution of group
dynamics as we create counter-storytelling community and move
through the four story types. Drawing on group dynamics and intergroup dialogue theories, I trace the evolution of counter-storytelling
community as the group explores the different story types and highlight the emotional and intellectual insights expressed by participants
at key points in the process.[1]

Group Dynamics and Intergroup Dialogue

The theory of small group dynamics developed by Tuckman and Jensen (1977) provides one useful way to show the evolution of storytelling community and make sense of how participants respond to the Storytelling Project Model. Tuckman and Jensen's theory posits that groups typically move through five stages: forming, storming, norming, performing and transforming, as outlined in Figure 6.1.

The *forming* stage is the ice breaking or getting acquainted stage when a group first comes together. In this initial stage, group members tend to be polite and cautious as they determine the purpose for gathering, feel each other out and tentatively explore what their own role might be. At this stage, participants tend to play it safe and usually avoid controversy or open disagreement. The task for facilitators includes providing an explicit agenda and creating an atmosphere where members feel welcome and invited to participate and express themselves honestly.

The group enters the next state, *storming*, when inevitable differences in ideas, opinions and perspectives arise and participants must work out ways to address disagreement, controversy and conflict.

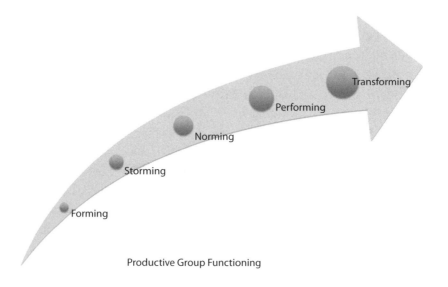

Figure 6.1 Small Group Dynamics (Tuckman & Jensen, 1977)

Facilitators can help by acknowledging the inevitability of conflict and its value for group learning and by helping participants develop norms for addressing disagreements and differences to work together productively. The third stage, *norming*, occurs as group members enact the norms established for working together and begin to experience themselves as a cohesive group with trustworthy members. Facilitators can help by reinforcing norms that help the group work together constructively to air and resolve disagreements and differences. In the *performing* stage, group members have established a sense of unity and are able to be highly productive together and engage with new ideas and challenges to move learning forward. The final stage, *transforming*, happens as the group experience comes to an end. The group moves toward closure and a sense of completion where participants recognize and appreciate what they have accomplished together. Facilitators can help by explicitly inviting participants to comment on the process of their work and give each other feedback and appreciation.

The theory posits that a group may be blocked at any stage in the process and not move forward. For example, a group whose members are too conforming or mistrustful may never move beyond the initial watchful stage as members fail to take the risks needed to move learning forward in the group. Or a group can become mired in conflict when there is not enough trust, skill or commitment to engage with and work through challenges that inevitably arise, and thus not be productive or feel satisfied with their work together.

When we add race and other hierarchically structured social positions (such as class, gender, sexuality, ability, age) these stages take on added weight as the group negotiates asymmetric relations of power and historically/socially embedded patterns of interaction. Here, intergroup dialogue theories provide additional insights for understanding group dynamics in diverse communities (Schoem & Hurtado, 2001; Zuniga, Nagda, Chesler & Cytron-Walker, 2007; Zuniga, Nagda & Sevig, 2002). Romney (2005, p. 7) summarizes five key points central to my discussion here:

> 1) People enter into dialogue *both* as individuals *and* as members of social identity groups; 2) power, privilege and historical/institutional oppression (recognized or unrecognized, acknowledged or not acknowledged)

are threads weaving through all dialogue among diverse groups; 3) moving from polite or angry talk to meaningful engagement requires time and a carefully structured process which encourages questioning and reflection; 4) dialogue facilitators need not be neutral, but should act as catalysts whose questions and probes deepen the dialogue; and 5) effective dialogue involves thinking and feeling, listening and learning, as well as talking.

The first two points underscore the role that social group membership and relations of power and privilege in the broader society always play in the dynamics of a diverse group and thus require attention for a group to be productive. The latter three points refer to process issues that affect how a group made up of diverse members will function and to conditions for productive dialogue. These include a carefully structured process that enables questioning and reflection, and facilitators who will push participants to engage with each other in honest and thoughtful ways through conscious self-awareness and careful listening. The goal is to enable participants to be aware of what they bring to the dialogue from both their individual and group experiences, remain open to multiple voices and perspectives, and consider what they can learn from a spirit of "appreciative inquiry" and "responsive understanding" (Romney, 2005). Below I explore these issues in the five-day, intensive summer institute focusing on the group dynamics and intergroup dialogue, and highlighting key issues that surfaced as we explored the four story types.

Day 1: Forming Counter-Storytelling Community

At the heart of the Storytelling Model is the creation of counter-storytelling community in which race and racism can be openly discussed in a diverse group and in which risks can be taken to expose how systemic racism operates in our daily lives and our role in supporting or resisting racial patterns. This initial step in the model pays conscious and proactive attention to the forming stage of group dynamics and to acknowledging the role that social group membership and social hierarchy play in interactions with others.[2] We open the institute by affirming these purposes and involve the group in activities where they can get to know one another, enter the topic of race and racism, and collectively consider and commit to explicit guidelines for our work together.[3]

Interactive activities that include movement and interaction unsettle expectations that participants will sit passively and listen to experts and encourage people to interact with each other in a playful and fairly low risk way. They provide a way to draw out shared experiences and interests as the first step in creating a web of connection that can hold differences and challenges that arise later.

In the Institute we draw on shared experiences of teaching to introduce storytelling genres and devices. Small groups of three to four people co-construct a story for advising an incoming group of novice teachers about what to expect on their first day of teaching. Drawing upon memories of what it is like to be a novice teacher each group creates a collective story. To add to the challenge each group draws from a hat slips of paper listing a vehicle for telling their story (puppets, rap song, poem, collage or dance) and a genre/purpose (comedy to entertain, mystery to frighten, romance to invite, science fiction to question, and soap opera to exaggerate). Each group then performs their story using the vehicle and genre/purpose, with much head-nodding recognition, laughter and applause. This activity introduces the topic of storytelling and lays the foundation for working with story types and different artistic genres and stimulates thinking about different methods of storytelling and the many ways a story can be expressed and adapted to an audience to serve various purposes. It also requires people to move out of their comfort zone and take a shared risk in front of peers as each group dramatizes its story.

After more formal introductions (such as name, subject taught, school, and something that intrigued them about this institute), and an overview of the Storytelling Project Model and story types, we turn to the topic of race and racism through an activity that asks participants to take a public stance on a series of statements. Participants are asked to physically place themselves along a continuum from "True for Me," "Don't Know," "Not True for Me" in response to statements such as: "You feel connected to the country from which your ancestors came," "You speak a language other than English at home," "You worry about discrimination in your community," "You have felt racial tension in a situation and were afraid to say anything about it."[4] Participants move silently and publicly to a position on the continuum after each question and then discuss with a person nearby why they placed themselves so. We point out that people may move to the same location for quite different reasons and ask participants to notice assumptions made on the basis of appearance or stance. We encourage them to pay attention to and consider the sources of their own thoughts, feelings and questions as these arise in dialogue with others. We also discuss how the stances we take are affected by our experiences both as individuals and as members of different social identity groups.

We introduce the concepts of *comfort zone* and *learning edge* (Griffin, 2007) as tools for tuning in to one's own feelings and reactions as well as for paying attention to others in the room. Comfort zone refers to playing it safe and holding on to what is comfortable and therefore not really challenging. Learning edge refers to taking risks to consider new perspectives and ideas. We encourage participants to use these concepts to push their learning edge and consciously take risks to learn something new. Participants anonymously write on index cards their hopes and fears about discussing racism in a racially diverse group. These are shuffled and redistributed so that each person receives a different card to read aloud. The statements become the basis for developing explicit guidelines to help group members define their learning edge, deal with fears openly and take risks in order to learn from others' perspectives, experiences and ideas.

The forming stage is critical to the creation of counter-storytelling community. Taking the time to build connections and notice both commonalities and differences provides a strong foundation for creating intentional community in which members can be attentive to racial issues, open to what others have to say and willing to accept challenges to their thinking. We explicitly name problems that often arise in groups where asymmetrical relations of power reflected in the broader society are likely to be reproduced. For example, white people often stay in a comfort zone that expects people of color to teach them about race, while people of color, fearing that their honest thoughts and feelings about racism will be dismissed or downplayed, curb their responses instead of openly expressing what they want to say. We also point out that risk and comfort are relative—what may seem comfortable for one person can feel extremely risky for another—and are affected by social position and power. We note that power dynamics are complicated by the fact that our subject positions are partial and multiple and that each of us is a complex of social identities that mediate our experience of the world and the degree of risk we face as members of advantaged/disadvantaged groups. Racial identity is always complicated and shaped by gender, class, sexual orientation, and other aspects of identity. While we foreground race, we need to also note the background identities that inflect experiences of race and racism, the partiality of our subject positions as participants and the relative nature of risk. We ask participants to notice and consciously track feelings as the week progresses as clues to whether they are playing it safe or staying on a learning edge. We discuss how we might operate in ways that do not reproduce the status quo but rather encourage us to stay open to ambiguity and paradox, so that we can embrace contradictions as seeds for developing a more critical consciousness about racism in our society.

While the concepts of "comfort zone" and "learning edge" provide a common language for recognizing and working with discomfort, the arts inevitably move us out of comfort with the known, create mind/body connections and new awareness, and offer different metaphors for examining beliefs and experiences with racism. The time spent on discussing how we will work together through consciously developing norms that encourage dialogue, careful listening and shared risk-taking will serve the group well as we move into more challenging material about race and racism.

Participants confirm the value of explicitly addressing the forming stage of group development and the emerging conditions for counter-storytelling community in their feedback at the end of the first day:

People were much more honest when writing their hopes and fears on an index card than talking in front of a group of people about race. When people speak everyone seems like they don't want to offend or hurt but on paper they were more truthful.

The most important thing I learned is that it is OK—people generally want to talk about racism. It is not something to be feared as long as there are guidelines and agreement of behaviors established.

One participant notes a willingness to be open to new perspectives and also identifies a learning edge in how difficult this will be:

> A statement that struck me the most from one of the participants is, "Humor is offensive." I never really put a lot of thought into it but now I see how that can happen. Even though we came up with guidelines about how to become more open-minded, I still feel that it is very hard for me to become more open-minded and self-aware.

Another appreciates the connections beginning to develop among participants:

> Creating new bonds with other highly creative individuals and sharing our experience [was a high point of the day].

To set the stage for stock stories, at the end of the day we provide copies of the DVD "Race: The Power of an Illusion" (Adelman, 2003) for participants to watch at home (and to keep for their own classroom use). This DVD shows the power of images and stories to name and challenge erroneous but popularly accepted (stock) stories about race, including the very legitimacy of race as a biological category. The DVD also reveals less well-known (concealed) stories about how race and white privilege have been constructed through law, government policy and social practice. The DVD generates surprising information for many and provokes dissonance for some as it challenges taken for granted notions about race and racism people bring to the table.

Day 2: Stock Stories—Forming to Storming

We begin the second day by surfacing areas of disagreement or differences of opinion as participants discuss reactions to the DVD: "What surprised you? What assumptions were challenged? What feelings, confusions or questions arose for you? How would you define race and racism based on what you learned?" We introduce the story type of stock stories as participants join discussion groups for identifying stock stories about race in the DVD.

The format of *Conversation Café* sets up multiple discussion options around café tables with coffee and cookies. Each table has a different question written on a sign in the middle of the table. Participants can join any one of four conversations, knowing that there will be three rounds and an option to either move to a new table/topic in each round or remain with the same table/topic. The conversation topics we used are:[5]

1) What is the difference between a biological and a social view of race? How have biological assumptions about race become taken for granted "common knowledge"? How might these assumptions be challenged?
2) How has whiteness been defined historically? What purposes have changing definitions of whiteness served in American society? To whose benefit?
3) Why do the stories we tell about race matter? What purposes do they serve? How do we negotiate the fallacy of biological race with the reality of race as lived experience?
4) What stories are erased, trivialized or concealed by the dominant story? How does this happen?

These discussions draw out opinions and ideas about race, racism and white advantage; surface disagreements, questions and confusions for further exploration; and develop shared knowledge about patterns and practices through which racism functions historically and today.

To complicate and further unsettle stock stories, artists on the team lead participants through a series of theater games (Boal, 2002) using generative words and phrases from the morning discussion: "power," "domination," "segregation," "resistance," "whiteness." In groups of three to four, participants create a series of tableaux in which they nonverbally position their bodies to represent still images of each term. Observers comment on the image and offer their interpretations. At different points, individuals step into the tableaux to alter the image and inject different meaning. Through stepping in to participate and standing back to observe, group members explore emotional connections and associations with racism, open up taken for granted ideas about how racism works, and consider how location/position differentially affect individuals and the meanings drawn from different tableaux.

Small groups meet separately to create an embodied way to enact a term or concept for the rest of the group: *racism, social construction, prejudice, discrimination,* and *white privilege.* The ensuing performances physicalize what participants have drawn from the previous activity. Participants begin to cohere as a group through taking risks, openly discussing disagreements and considering alternative perspectives.[6]

> *The low point of the day was feeling a sense of discomfort … the most important thing I learned was that discomfort has the opportunity to bring forth change.*

> *The most important thing I learned today was being much more aware of what I don't have to think about as a white person.*

> *I learned a lot from the conversation café but I was frustrated at not having answers for all of the questions. I have more questions than answers right now.*

> *It's hard to share your experience without generalizing, but important to do so.*

> *To see each group compile their talents, thoughts and knowledge was wonderful! Also the story café was so intimate and brought out so much I could never have known. The assigned readings are always wonderful—the video was so informative—I can't wait to use it to interact with my students.*

Day 3: Concealed Stories—Storming to Norming

As homework and to introduce the idea of concealed stories, participants are asked: *"Bring an artifact/physical object that represents race in your life; something that is personal/special and that you wouldn't mind sharing with the group and would allow other people to touch or handle it."* The next morning they arrive with their artifacts and are invited to place them somewhere in the room that seems appropriate. Once all the artifacts have been placed, they silently walk around and observe the display. Next, again silently, they create collections of pieces that seem to belong together. Some silent struggle occurs as disagreements arise and have to be nonverbally negotiated to establish what items should be placed where. Once collections are arranged, participants form small groups around each collection of artifacts and create a story about the meaning and significance of the collection. Each group relates their completed story to the whole group. Individuals then have the opportunity to respond to the placement and rendering of the artifact they brought and to clarify and/or contradict interpretations that have been made about their piece. This process of clarification introduces concealed stories and raises questions about what it is like to expose a personally meaningful story and have it interpreted, or misinterpreted, by others. One participant says:

Sharing the artifacts and stories and having people understand was powerful. I often feel misunderstood and I was impressed how the class community embraced me.

Another notes,

The high point was sharing the artifacts. I think it was a very sensitive activity for all of us and helped us to understand the power of concealed stories that we often don't share with others.

The exploration of concealed stories continues as Rosemarie Roberts and Roger Bonair-Agard, artists who worked on the Echoes Project, show and discuss pieces from the DVD "Echoes of Brown" (Fine et al., 2004) of youth reading original poetry about their experiences and frustrations in school. One poem read by two young women, one Latina the other white, challenges the hypocrisy of their school's public image as integrated in the context of its pervasive practices of tracking and exclusion. A second poem, read by an African American young man, relates his experiences of shame, confusion and anger at having to sit in the balcony with other "special ed" students while his girlfriend sits in the auditorium below. He compares tracking in special education to racial segregation and describes how an encouraging teacher who taught him African American history helped him discover his own previously unrecognized capacities. His poem is provocative, poised, deeply moving and eloquently critical. Some participants comment, "He can't be Special Ed!" leading us to unpack what this suggests about the stereotypes and assumptions that govern how certain students are viewed and treated in our educational system.

Participants discuss these evocative poems in small groups, identify the concealed stories about education and race reflected in the poems and comment on the challenges these young people raise for them as teachers. Each participant then writes a poem or short story about race and education in which they respond to youth concerns from a teacher's perspective. Volunteers read their pieces aloud to the whole group. Some teachers find it quite challenging to consider how racial ideas and stereotypes affect how students are tracked and labeled in schools. They clearly find themselves on a learning edge as they witness the world through the eyes of students so affected and consider their role as teachers in either perpetuating or challenging these practices.

These explorations lead to an examination of white privilege/advantage, beginning with the "crossing the room" activity using the list of privileges developed by Peggy McIntosh (McIntosh, 1990). In our version, we ask participants to hold hands and try to maintain connection, as individuals step forward for each statement that is true for them: "Move forward if schools in your community teach about your race and heritage in positive ways throughout the year," "Move forward if you can go shopping and be assured most of the time that you will not be followed because of your race," "Move forward if you never have to think twice about calling the police when trouble occurs."[7] Inevitably, the distance between white participants and participants of color increases, eventually forcing people to let go of each other's hands. In an immediate and physical way this activity illustrates the disruption of community that is created by unequal advantages based on race. Participants discuss their feelings and reactions to the exercise and whether individuals considered resisting or refusing to participate. We discuss stock stories that rationalize and encourage those who benefit from unearned advantages to feel OK about moving forward, unaware of or ignoring what is happening to those left behind. Several participants find this a personally powerful and revealing activity. White participants comment on the visceral recognition of how white advantage operates, often out of conscious awareness, but with very real consequences in the lives of others. Participants of color note the usefulness of literally seeing and naming patterns and practices they experience that are so often denied or underplayed by mainstream society.

We replay Part III of the DVD "Race: The Power of an Illusion," which illustrates how white advantage is constructed in law and public policy. The fishbowl discussion following the DVD proves to be a critical moment when the value of our guidelines becomes apparent. An African American woman speaks tearfully about her shock at discovering the degree to which racial advantage and disadvantage are constructed, newly recognizing ways that her own life has been affected. Before she can finish, a white participant interrupts and asserts that she too has experienced disadvantage and that the problem is really class not race. One can feel the entire room hold its collective breath. Clearly this is a crucial moment. Will we move on with the discussion, as often happens, smoothing over tension and disagreement? Instead one of the facilitators quietly asks the white participant to repeat what she heard her African American colleague say. When she cannot do so, it becomes clear that she had tuned out the first speaker.

By pausing the action and preserving space for the first woman to fully express what she wants to say, the white participant is able to hear her and take in the pain, anger and sorrow embodied in her response. The group experiences what can open up when we interrupt and bracket patterned interactions and take the time to analyze them more fully. In this instance, pausing and rewinding the conversation enables the group to consider how white people when they are uncomfortable with discussions of racism often interrupt people of color and re-center their own concerns. The group discusses how this pattern reflects the privilege of ignoring the pain of racism, reinforcing white numbness and lack of awareness or focus on the uncomfortable dynamics of positional power. Through the discussion participants become more conscious about naming this pattern when it arises so as to interrupt it and change the dynamic.

Once the group fully acknowledges the first speaker, understanding the connections she has made between information in the DVD and the racial underpinnings of her experience, it becomes possible to turn to the reactions of the second speaker. We are able to help her figure out what in the DVD triggered her feelings and reactions and have a grounded discussion of the experiences of guilt and denial that exposure to racial privilege so often evokes, as well as examine the confounding experiences of class that inflect racial experience.

By freezing the action and taking the time to unpack triggering comments we can more clearly pinpoint differences in perspectives and be more attentive to racial positionality, intersecting aspects of social identity, and individual experiences as they affect intergroup dialogue. This discussion proves to be a pivotal turning point for the group as participants are called upon to listen across racial experiences with greater care, to examine how racial positionality impacts their ability to listen to and learn from one another, to own their ability to either collude in or interrupt such practices, and to explore more deeply patterns we typically take for granted or pass over that enable racism to continue.

As participants write about their learning edge they speak to the impact of the activities and discussions from this pivotal third day:

The low point of my day was the fishbowl. I felt uncomfortable and pissed off that people still don't get it. I wanted to cry but tears don't prove any points. Funny enough my learning edge was the fishbowl. Go figure. The thing that made me want to scream and cry was relevant. That is the point. And yet I still found myself silencing myself because I don't want to be seen as bitter and unreachable.

Why do we choose to remain silent?

Realizing the privileges I experience from being white! Knowing now what the government has done to us!

Seeing people in our group realize that there is whiteness.

Getting too uncomfortable seems to be OK.

Being able to be honest and open and not feel like I offended anyone.

I learned that patience is needed and that this struggle is not a quick fix.

Summative evaluations at the conclusion of the five-day institute also recalled this particular day, the third day, as marking a turning point for participants—in their willingness to take risks with one another, express disagreement thoughtfully but invite new perspectives, and consciously and openly work through tensions that arise.

Day 4: Resistance Stories—Norming to Performing

By the fourth day of the institute, the group has begun to take more risks, to act on norms of honesty and careful listening, address racial positionality and acknowledge privilege and disadvantage, and work through disagreements and divergent perspectives in ways that open up new learning. We turn to an exploration of resistance stories through the practices of various artists, including the artists on our creative team.

Rosemarie Roberts, drawing on her experience as a dancer, begins with video clips of African dances, tracing their historical uses in slave society to covertly express resistance where overt resistance was deadly. She engages the group in learning some aspects of African dance, an activity that pushes everyone to a learning edge as the physicality of dance, awkward for most of us, provides both a shared experience of vulnerability and the smallest glimpse into how dance can express covert and overt resistance to racial domination. This attunes the group to the many ways that resistance can operate and the variety of ways it can be expressed.

Roger Bonair-Agard performs a dramatic reading of his poetry, sharing two powerful and moving pieces, one about his mother's instructions to her black male child about how to negotiate a racist world, the other about his experience as the only black person in a bar with a group of white friends when a racial epithet is directed at him, and no one says a word. The poems are direct, angry and powerful, asserting Roger's refusal to quell or silence the truths of his experiences as a black man. He provokes his listeners to consider our own silence as witnesses, and the collusion with racism that occurs when people stand by and let it happen without comment. We experience at a visceral level how doing nothing is all that is required to keep racism going, and the terrible cost inflicted on others when we do so.

Kayhan Irani performs a segment from her one-woman show in which she dramatizes the experiences of various people in NYC following 9/11. We watch Kayhan become a Sikh woman responding to an angry phone call from a white man who claims he will bomb her temple (confusing her religion and ethnicity in his search for someone to blame). She transforms into a young Arab girl whose father is taken off for questioning and never returns. With a change of stance and voice she becomes a white guard at a detention center (where Arab men have been told to line up) who feels compelled to comment on the injustice of treating innocent people as terrorists simply based on skin color or national origin. Through these characters, Kayhan inspires her audience to resist simplistic stories and images, to empathize with the individual and collective plight of others we do not know, and to respond emotionally to the injustice of their treatment. We are invited into a visceral experience of resistance through art forms that call out and challenge racism and provoke us to consider our own action/inaction and collusion when we remain silent.

In recognition of brimming and often divergent emotions following these performances—for white participants guilt, fear, numbness; and participants of color anger, sadness, frustration—we separate into caucus groups by race led by same-race facilitators. The caucus groups provide an opportunity to express feelings and reactions in response to the performances they have witnessed and to begin a discussion of resistance to racism with members of their own racial group. Despite initial hesitation, participants unanimously conclude that, while uncomfortable—especially for the white group—this is another important learning/turning point. Participants say they are able to express thoughts, feelings, questions and confusions shared by other members of their racial group and help each other think about how they might constructively act on their feelings to resist racism. When we reconvene as a whole, each small group spends twenty minutes or so in a fishbowl surrounded by the other group, and summarizes highlights from their discussion while the other group listens quietly.

In their evaluations at the end of the day, members from both groups name the caucus groups as both challenging and a high point of the day:

The high point of the day was the caucus group because it gave an arena for concerns that could probably be heard better [in "same race" groups].

When we broke up into groups we got to express a lot about the legacy of colonialism and slavery.

The high point was the caucus groups. I was able to speak much more freely than in the whole group.

The high point of the day was the caucus group. The group discussion resolved some issues about which I was confused.

The caucus group really worked for me because the facilitators addressed issues that personally affected me.

To bring the day to a close and think more personally about resistance, each participant creates a collage that tells a story of resistance to racism either in her/his own life or through a historical example that is meaningful as a guide for what they might do in the future. Participant feedback indicates that not only do the collages help them think about the forms of resistance stories, they also find the exercise personally meaningful and a source of useful ideas for how to incorporate resistance stories in their classrooms and personal lives. Several cite a chapter from Race Rebels (Kelley, 1996), a reading from the previous evening's homework that clarifies the notion of resistance and feeds into the performance aspect of the day. They also express pleasure in creatively integrating what they have learned to create their own resistance collage:

Making the collage was a high point. At first I thought I wouldn't be able to come up with anything for the collage, but once I got started I had a real message of resistance that I wanted to share.

A high point was creating the collages. The feedback and presentation of the art pieces was wonderful and expressive.

The collage was powerful. We are all creative and we all have stories of resistance that are different but that we can all relate to.

Constructing the collage was great. It helped me express my views on resistance and helped me see if people understood what I was trying to say.

I enjoyed the whole day but especially the collage because it gave me a chance to express myself artistically.

For most participants, the same-race caucus groups are especially meaningful. They note that speaking with members of their own racial group helps them express feelings and confusions and gain support that enables them to feel more open to and prepared for crossracial group discussions. A running theme as we close is also anxiety about how all of the issues we have opened up for discussion will reach resolution with only one day remaining.

Day 5: Emerging/Transforming Stories—Performing to Transforming

On the final day of the institute we turn to emerging/transforming storytelling as participants develop and present action plans to apply what they have learned from the institute back home in their classrooms, schools and personal lives. Participants bring in drafts of action plans developed at home the previous evening and share these in small groups to get feedback and support from peers. After revising and elaborating further, they share their plans in the broader group and receive more suggestions and feedback. They end up with a fairly well-developed sequence of steps that they commit to enacting back home in their schools and communities. Examples include: development of new lessons in English and Social Studies that focus on the social construction of race in American History and literature and using the four story types to engage students in critical analysis of stock stories; a plan for working with students and colleagues to proactively surface and address racial issues in their schools by creating counter-storytelling communities where talking critically about race and racism is invited and supported; personal action plans to continue to develop their own knowledge about racism through further reading, courses and conversations.

Participants see these action plans as the impetus for taking a stance against racism and positioning themselves as responsible agents of change. They appreciate the opportunity to think about and plan next steps and see this is an important part of gaining closure for the institute while maintaining momentum to continue the work beyond.

I really felt a connection to the project and incorporating my action plan. Thank you for this experience of awareness.

Presenting and getting feedback on my action plan was such a great feeling.

I love listening to the presentations. To me, this is very important because you hear the actions of how each of us will be implementing to make the world, or our classroom, a better place to be in. I love that the facilitators showed us, shared their work with us.

In final evaluations, teachers write about connections between individual high and low points and learning edges. The majority of participants focus their comments around Day 3's activities—what I have called the storming to norming stage. Several list this day as both the low and high point for the week; low because of the discomfort and tension related to misunderstandings and conflicts in the room and high because engaging these tensions pushes them to their learning edge and moves them to reexamine racism on a far deeper level. The storming process seems to have incorporated conditions for honest intergroup dialogue and propelled movement into the norming and performing stages to open up deeper learning.

Another high/low example mentioned in evaluations is the final project. Though a few participants express frustration at time constraints and confusion about the form of the project, they are ultimately pleased with the final presentations. Reflecting on the concept of learning edge, a few people make direct connections about how to bring the Storytelling Project Model into their own classrooms to invite students to critically examine racism in literature, art, history, music and other subjects.

Most of the learning edges described by participants speak to the individual and collective journey they have taken during the week. Mentioned as key are: learning about white privilege and seeing how it works in their lives; drawing on resistance stories to consider purposeful actions they can take to address racial dynamics and racism in their classrooms and schools; dealing with anger and frustration and working towards a productive solution in a racially diverse group; realizing one's own prejudices and limitations, and the most frequently stated learning edge—a challenge to not stay silent and to continue to work towards making a difference in their schools, classrooms and personal lives. These reflections speak to a sense of resolution, even transformation that brings the group to closure but with ongoing reverberations for new action in their personal and professional lives going forward.

Participants describe the Storytelling Project Model as a valuable tool for analyzing racial issues and for personalizing an understanding of systemic racism. Through learning about the different kinds of stories, they say it is easier to dissect stereotypes, take responsibility for addressing racism and think about concrete ways to take action. One participant discusses the sense of personal ownership that talking about racism through stories creates. Others talk about how much clearer the problem of racism becomes when it has a human face and that stories and story types provide a lens for seeing and addressing racism more directly.

Conclusion

I have focused here on the process of creating a counter-storytelling community in which productive discussions about race and racism in a racially diverse group can occur, drawing on group dynamics and intergroup dialogue theories as an organizing frame. I have also referenced arts-based activities through which we approach different story types—specifically poetry, dance, drama, theater games and collage. As facilitators, we learned a great deal from this first unveiling of the Storytelling Project Model. We could see that the arts play an important role in building a community where risks can be taken and shared, and new norms established for acting against racism. We learned that experiencing the arts directly can be transformative for helping people look at racism within themselves and in the broader society in more honest and meaningful ways. From participant feedback we also learned that the Storytelling Project Model makes sense to people and offers useful guidelines and strategies for teachers to take back into their own personal lives and the classrooms and schools where they teach.

We also learned that constant vigilance and courage are required to challenge patterns of domination and subordination. The guidelines must be called upon and used the very first time they are forgotten or violated, or participants will distrust the process and pull back to safer ground. It takes time to build community in which risks can be taken, but devoting time to this task is essential. We also learned that teachers need lots of support and information about stock and concealed stories, about how to use the arts in their teaching, and about how to make sense of their own racial positionality. Many teachers are eager for this knowledge and willing to take risks to learn about and find ways to act against racism in their classrooms and lives. They see the Storytelling Project Model as a useful framework for motivating commitment and generating action. Ideally, teachers who hold these commitments can create counter-storytelling communities in their schools, among colleagues and with students, parents and community groups; communities that can help them sustain the vision and persistence to go against the grain of stock stories, uncover concealed stories, draw lessons from resistance stories and generate emerging/transforming stories that can lead us toward a more just society shaped by all of us as active and valued citizens.

Notes

Chapter 1

1   This chapter is based on the collaborative work of the Storytelling Project Creative Team and especially my collaborative work with Rosemarie Roberts.

2   In earlier writing about the model, we labeled the fourth story type "counter-stories" but then I realized that except for stock stories the other three story types are forms of counter-story. So here I have changed the label from counter-stories to emerging/transforming stories. This change also illustrates more clearly, I hope, that these stories emerge from the understanding of history and structure we gain from studying concealed and resistance stories and build on those story types.

Chapter 3

1   We looked at several contemporary artists and a list of their work can be found in the Storytelling Project Curriculum. Other images can be found in Lippard (1984, 1990) and PBS (2007).

Chapter 4

1   The quotations in this section are from unpublished research notes resulting from a study undertaken by Roberts, Bell and Murphy (2005–2006), some of which are presented in Roberts et al. (2008, pp. 334–354).

2   Many excellent sources for such poems exist. We have used Leslie Marmon Silko, Langston Hughes and Pedro Pietri among others.

Chapter 5

1   Thea Abu El-Haj, a member of the creative team, introduced us to this speech and the close reading process.

2   Several valuable networks of support for teachers do exist. For example: NYCORE—New York Collective of Radical Teachers (www.nycore.org) and Rethinking Schools (www.rethinkingschools.org) to name two. The Barnard Education Program has developed a New Teacher Network for this purpose that is linked to teacher support networks in Boston and Philadelphia created by CETE—Consortium for Excellence in Teacher Education.

Chapter 6

1   **Background:** In summer 2005, we offered a weeklong summer insti-
    tute for educators in New York City to introduce the Storytelling Proj-
    ect Model and test its accessibility and usefulness for teachers. Teachers
    throughout the city were invited to sign up for the institute and could
    receive in-service credit through the New York City Department of Edu-
    cation. We asked participants to fill out a questionnaire about their inter-
    ests in and knowledge of racism prior to the institute to help us assess
    their entering knowledge and to build activities around their questions
    and concerns. Given our limited space and our desire to build community
    in which risks could be taken, we closed the institute at twenty partici-
    pants. The group was a diverse mix of elementary and secondary teachers
    (though primarily secondary), with one librarian and one social worker
    who taught incarcerated youth. The group was about one-third male and
    two-thirds female, and included Whites, Blacks, Asians and Latinos.
        Five members of the creative team facilitated the five-day institute,
    two artists (Kayhan Irani and Roger Bonair-Agard) and three educa-
    tors (myself, Rosemarie Roberts and Zoe Duskin). Two student interns
    (Brett Murphy and Ebonie Smith) documented our work as we pro-
    ceeded by keeping notes and videotaping parts of the proceedings. We
    met in the same generative space where the creative team had worked so
    productively when we were developing the model and we used many of
    the activities developed and honed further in our work together. We met
    for eight hours a day, Monday through Friday, for a very intensive week
    of exploration and engagement.
2   The Storytelling Summer Institute for New York City teachers deliber-
    ately sought a racially diverse group of teachers and the facilitation team
    was equally diverse.
3   Many of the activities we designed are available in the Storytelling Proj-
    ect Curriculum. A free downloadable PDF is available at www.barnard.
    edu/education/storytelling.
4   A version of this and the next activity is available in Bell, Love and Rob-
    erts (2007).
5   Adapted from the online guide accompanying the DVD, available from
    California Newsreel at www.californianewsreel.com.
6   All quotes are taken from evaluations participants completed at the end
    of each day of the institute and summary evaluations after the five-day
    institute.
7   See Bell, Love and Roberts (2007), Appendix D, for additional
    questions.

References

Adams, M., Bell, L.A., & Griffin, P. (Eds.). (2007). *Teaching for Diversity and Social Justice* (2nd ed.). New York: Routledge.

Adelman, L. (Writer) (2003). *Race: The Power of an Illusion* (DVD). California Newsreel.

Alcoff, L. (1998). What Should White People Do? *Hypatia, 13*(3), 6–26.

Allen, P.G. (1992). *The Sacred Hoop: Recovering the Feminine in American Indian Traditions, with a New Preface*. Boston, MA: Beacon Press.

Allen, P.G. (1996). *Song of the Turtle: American Indian Literature, 1974–1994*. New York: Ballantine Books.

Angelou, M. (1978). *And Still I Rise*. New York: Random House.

Anyon, J. (1997). *Ghetto Schooling: A Political Economy of Urban Education Reform*. New York: Teachers College Press.

Anzaldúa, G. (1990). *Making Face, Making Soul/Haciendo Caras: Creative and Critical Perspectives by Women of Color*. San Francisco, CA: Aunt Lute Books.

Anzaldúa, G. (2007). *Borderlands/La Frontera: The New Mestiza* (3rd ed.). San Francisco, CA: Aunt Lute Books.

Apfelbaum, E.K. (2000). And Now What, After Such Tribulations?: Memory and Dislocation in the Era of Uprooting. *American Psychologist, 55*(9), 1008–1013.

Aptheker, H. (1992). *Anti-Racism in U.S. History: The First Two Hundred Years*. New York: Greenwood Press.

Atlas, C., & Korza, P. (Eds.). (2005). *Critical Perspectives: Writing on Art and Civic Dialogue*. Washington, DC: Americans for the Arts.

Bambara, T.C., & Morrison, T. (1996). *Deep Sightings and Rescue Missions: Fiction, Essays, and Conversations*. New York: Pantheon Books.

Banks, J.A. (2002). Teaching for Diversity and Unity in a Democratic Multicultural Society. In W.C. Parker (Ed.), *Education for Democracy: Contexts, Curricula, Assessments* (pp. 131–150). Greenwich, CT: Information Age.

Barlow, A.L. (2003). *Between Fear and Hope: Globalization and Race in the United States*. Lanham, MD: Rowman & Littlefield.

Bell, D. (2009). Who's Afraid of Critical Race Theory? In E. Taylor, D. Gillborn & G. Ladson-Billings (Eds.), *Foundations of Critical Race Theory in Education* (pp. 37–50). New York: Routledge.

Bell, D.A. (1989). *And We Are Not Saved: The Elusive Quest for Racial Justice*. New York: Basic Books.

Bell, D.A. (1992). *Faces at the Bottom of the Well: The Permanence of Racism*. New York: Basic Books.

Bell, D.A., Delgado, R., & Stefancic, J. (2005). *The Derrick Bell Reader*. New York: New York University Press.

Bell, L.A. (2003a). Telling Tales: What Stories Can Teach Us about Race and Racism. *Race, Ethnicity and Education, 6*(1), 3–28.

Bell, L.A. (2003b). Sincere Fictions: The Challenges of Preparing White Teachers for Diverse Classrooms. *Equity and Excellence in Education, 35*(3), 236–245.

Bell, L.A. (2007). Theoretical Foundations for Social Justice Education. In M. Adams, L.A. Bell & P. Griffin (Eds.), *Teaching for Diversity and Social Justice* (2nd ed., pp. 3–15). New York: Routledge.

Bell, L.A. (2010). Learning through Story Types about Race and Racism: Preparing Teachers for Social Justice. In K. Skubikowski, C. Wright & R. Graf (Eds.), *Social Justice Education: Inviting Faculty to Change Institutions.* Sterling, VA: Stylus Publishing.

Bell, L.A., Joshi, K., & Zuniga, X. (2007). Racism and Immigration. In M. Adams, L.A. Bell & P. Griffin (Eds.), *Teaching for Diversity and Social Justice* (2nd ed., pp. 145–166). New York: Routledge.

Bell, L.A., Love, B.J., & Roberts, R.A. (2007). Racism and White Privilege Curriculum Design. In M. Adams, L.A. Bell & P. Griffin (Eds.), *Teaching for Diversity and Social Justice* (2nd ed., pp. 123–144). New York: Routledge.

Bell, L.A., & Roberts, R.A. (2010). The Storytelling Project Model: A Theoretical Framework for a Critical Examination of Racism through the Arts. *Teachers College Record, 112*(9), http://www.tcrecord.org.

Bell, L.A., Roberts, R.A., Irani, K., & Murphy, B. (2008). *The Storytelling Project Curriculum: Learning about Race and Racism through Storytelling and the Arts.* Unpublished curriculum, Barnard College, Columbia University, New York.

Berger, M. (1999). *White Lies: Race and the Myths of Whiteness.* New York: Farrar, Straus and Giroux.

Blackmon, D.A. (2008). *Slavery By Another Name: The Re-Enslavement of Black Americans from the Civil War to World War II.* New York: Doubleday.

Boal, A. (2001). *Theatre of the Oppressed.* New York: Theatre Communications Group, Inc.

Boal, A. (2002). *Games for Actors and Non-Actors* (2nd ed.). New York: Routledge.

Boler, M. (1999). *Feeling Power: Emotions and Education.* New York: Routledge.

Bonilla-Silva, E. (2001). *White Supremacy and Racism in the Post-Civil Rights Era.* Boulder, CO: Lynne Rienner Publishers.

Bonilla-Silva, E. (2003). "New Racism," Color-Blind Racism, and the Future of Whiteness in America. In A.W. Doane & E. Bonilla-Silva (Eds.), *White Out: The Continuing Significance of Racism* (pp. 271–284). New York: Routledge.

Bonilla-Silva, E. (2006a). *Racism Without Racists: Color-Blind Racism and the Persistence of Racial Inequality in the United States* (2nd ed.). Lanham, MD: Rowman & Littlefield.

Bonilla-Silva, E. (2006b). What is Racism?: The Racialized Social System Framework. In M.H. Durr & A. Shirley (Eds.), *Race, Work and Family in the Lives of African Americans* (pp. 13–43). Lanham, MD: Rowman & Littlefield.

Bonilla-Silva, E., Lewis, A., & Embrick, D.G. (2004). "I Did Not Get That Job Because Of a Black Man…": The Story Lines and Testimonies of Color-Blind Racism. *Sociological Forum, 19*(4), 555–581.

Brayboy, B.M.J. (2005a). Toward a Tribal Critical Race Theory in Education. *The Urban Review, 37*(5), 425–446.

Brayboy, B.M.J. (2005b). Transformational Resistance and Social Justice: American Indians in Ivy League Universities. *Anthropology and Education Quarterly, 36*(3), 192–211.

Brown, C.S. (2002). *Refusing Racism: White Allies and the Struggle for Civil Rights.* New York: Teachers College Press.

Bruner, J. (1996). *The Culture of Education.* Cambridge, MA: Harvard University Press.

Bullock, H., & Lott, B. (2006). Building a Research and Advocacy Agenda on Issues of Economic Justice. *Analyses of Social Issues and Public Policy, 1*(1), 147–162.

Bush, M. (2004). *Breaking the Code of Good Intentions: Everyday Forms of Whiteness.* Lanham, MD: Rowman & Littlefield.

Carroll, R. (1997). *Sugar in the Raw: Voices of Young Black Girls in America.* New York: Crown.

Center, A.R. (2009, May). *Race and Recession: How Inequity Rigged the Economy and How to Change the Rules.* New York: Applied Research Center.

Christensen, L. (2000). *Reading, Writing and Rising Up: Social Justice and the Power of the Written Word.* Milwaukee, WI: Rethinking Schools.

Christensen, L. (2009). *Teaching for Joy and Justice.* Milwaukee, WI: Rethinking Schools.

Churchill, W., & Trask, H.-K. (2005). *Since Predator Came: Notes from the Struggle for American Indian Liberation.* Edinburgh; Oakland, CA: AK Press.

Clover, D.E. (2006). Culture and Antiracisms in Adult Education: An Exploration of the Contributions of Arts-Based Learning. *Adult Education Quarterly, 57*(1), 46–61.

Cobas, J.A., & Feagin, J.R. (2007). Language Oppression and Resistance: The Case of Middle Class Latinos in the United States. *Ethnic and Racial Studies, 31*(2), 390–410.

Collier-Thomas, B., & Franklin, V.P. (2001). *Sisters in the Struggle: African American Women in the Civil Rights–Black Power Movement.* New York: New York University Press.

Comer, J.P. (2004). *Leave No Child Behind: Preparing Today's Youth for Tomorrow's World.* New Haven, CT: Yale University Press.

Cose, E. (1995). *The Rage of a Privileged Class.* New York: HarperPerennial.

Cose, E. (1997). *Color-Blind: Seeing Beyond Race in a Race-Obsessed World.* New York: HarperCollins Publishers.

Cowhey, M. (2006). *Black Ants and Buddhists: Thinking Critically and Teaching Differently in the Primary Grades*. Portland, ME: Stenhouse Publishers.

Dance, D.C. (2002). *From My People: 400 Years of African American Folklore*. New York: Norton.

Darling-Hammond, L. (1995). Inequality and Access to Knowledge. In J. Banks & C. McGee Banks (Eds.), *Handbook of Research on Multicultural Education* (pp. 465–483). New York: Macmillan.

Delgado, R. (1989). Storytelling for Oppositionists and Others: A Plea for Narrative. *Michigan Law Review, 87*, 2411–2441.

Delgado, R., & Stefancic, J. (1995). *Critical Race Theory: The Cutting Edge*. Philadelphia, PA: Temple University Press.

Deloria, V. (1995). *Red Earth, White Lies: Native Americans and the Myth of Scientific Fact*. New York: Scribner.

de los Reyes, E., & Gozemba, P. (2002). *Pockets of Hope: How Students and Teachers Change the World*. Westport, CT: Bergen & Garvey.

Derman-Sparks, L., Ramsey, P.G., & Edwards, J.O. (2006). *What If All the Kids Are White?: Anti-Bias, Multicultural Education with Young Children and Families*. New York: Teachers College Press.

Desai, D. (2000). Imaging Difference: The Politics of Representation in Multicultural Art Education. *Studies in Art Education, 41*(2), 114–129.

Desai, D., Hamlin, J., & Mattson, R. (2009). *History as Art, Art as History: Contemporary Art and Social Studies Education*. New York: Routledge.

Dixson, A.R., & Rousseau, C.K. (2006). *Critical Race Theory in Education: All God's Children Got a Song*. New York: Routledge.

Doane, A.W., & Bonilla-Silva, E. (2003). *White Out: The Continuing Significance of Racism*. New York: Routledge.

Draut, T. (2008). *The Economic State of Young America*. New York: Demos.

Dyer, R. (1997). *White*. New York: Routledge.

Eisner, E. (2002). *The Arts and the Creation of Mind*. New Haven, CT: Yale University Press.

El-Haj, T.R.A. (2007). "I Was Born Here But My Home, It's Not Here": Educating for Democratic Citizenship in an Era of Transnational Migration and Global Conflict. *Harvard Educational Review, 77*(3), 285–316.

El-Haj, T.R.A. (2009). Imagining Postnationalism: Arts, Citizenship Education, and Arab American Youth. *Anthropology and Education Quarterly, 40*(1), 1–19.

Epstein, T. (2009). *Interpreting National History: Race, Identity and Pedagogy in Classrooms and Communities*. New York: Routledge.

Erenreich, B., & Muhammad, D. (2009, September 13). The Recession's Racial Divide. *The New York Times*, p. 17.

Essed, P. (1991). *Understanding Everyday Racism: An Interdisciplinary Theory*. Newbury Park, CA: Sage Publications.

Ewick, P., & Silbey, S.S. (1995). Subversive Stories and Hegemonic Tales: Toward a Sociology of Narrative. *Law & Society Review, 29*(2), 197–226.

Feagin, J.R. (2001). *Racist America Roots, Current Realities, and Future Reparations*. New York; London: Routledge.

Feagin, J.R. (2006). *Systemic Racism: A Theory of Oppression*. New York: Routledge.

Feagin, J.R., & Sikes, M.P. (1994). *Living with Racism: The Black Middle-Class Experience*. Boston, MA: Beacon Press.

Fine, M. (1991). *Framing Dropouts: Notes on the Politics of an Urban Public High School*. New York: SUNY Press.

Fine, M. (1997). Off White: Readings on Race, Power, and Society. New York: Routledge.

Fine, M., Roberts, R.A., Torre, M.E., with Bloom, J., Burns, A. et al. (2004). *Echoes of Brown: Youth Documenting and Performing the Legacy of* Brown v Board of Education (DVD and accompanying book). New York: Teachers College Press.

Fisher, M. (2007). Every City Has Soldiers: The Role of Intergenerational Relationships in Participatory Literacy Communities. *Research in the Teaching of English, 42*(2), 139–162.

Foundation, S. (2009). *Lost Opportunity: A 50 State Report on the Opportunity to Learn in America*. Cambridge, MA: Schott Foundation for Public Education.

Frankenberg, R. (1993). *White Women, Race Matters: The Social Construction of Whiteness*. Minneapolis: University of Minnesota Press.

Frankenberg, R. (1997). *Displacing Whiteness: Essays in Social and Cultural Criticism*. Durham, NC: Duke University Press.

Freire, P., & Freire, A.M.A. (1994). *Pedagogy of Hope: Reliving Pedagogy of the Oppressed*. New York: Continuum.

Fuhrman, S., & Lazerson, M. (Eds.). (2005). *The Public Schools*. Oxford, UK: Oxford University Press.

Fulbright-Anderson, K., Lawrence, K., Sutton, S., Susi, G., & Kubisch, A. (2005). *Structural Racism and Youth Development: Issues, Challenges, and Implications*. Washington, DC: Aspen Institute.

Garvey, J., & Ignatiev, N. (1996). *Race Traitor*. New York: Routledge.

Ginwright, P., & Cammarota, J. (2006). Introduction. In S. Ginwright, P. Noguera & J. Cammarota (Eds.), *Beyond Resistance!: Youth Activism and Community Change* (pp. xiii–xxiii). New York: Routledge.

Giroux, H.A. (2003). *The Abandoned Generation: Democracy Beyond the Culture of Fear*. New York: Palgrave Macmillan.

Giroux, H.A. (2004). Class Casualties: Disappearing Youth in the Age of Market Fundamentalism. In *The Terror of Neoliberalism: Authoritarianism and the Eclipse of Democracy* (pp. 81–104). Boulder, CO: Paradigm.

Gordon, R., Della Piana, L., & Keleher, T. (1998). *Facing the Consequences: An Examination of Racial Discrimination in Public Schools*. Oakland, CA: Applied Research Center.

Gould, S.J. (1996). *The Mismeasure of Man* (Rev. and expanded ed.). New York: Norton.

Gramsci, A. (1971). *Selections from the Prison Notebooks of Antonio Gramsci*, edited and translated by Q. Hoare and G. Nowell Smith. London: Lawrence and Wishart.

Grande, S. (2004). *Red Pedagogy: Native American Social and Political Thought.* Lanham, MD: Rowman & Littlefield.

Green, J. (2000). *Taking History to Heart: The Power of the Past in Building Social Movements.* Amherst, MA: University of Massachusetts Press.

Greene, M. (1995). *Releasing the Imagination: Essays on Education, the Arts, and Social Change.* San Francisco, CA: Jossey-Bass.

Greene, M. (2004). *Imagination, Oppression and Culture: Creating Authentic Openings.* Paper presented at the Interrupting Oppression and Sustaining Justice Conference, New York.

Griffin, L.J. (2004). "Generations and Collective Memory" Revisited: Race, Region, and Memory of Civil Rights. *American Sociological Review, 69*(August), 544–557.

Griffin, P. (2007). Conceptual Foundations for Social Justice Education: Introductory Modules. In M. Adams, L.A. Bell & P. Griffin (Eds.), *Teaching for Diversity and Social Justice* (2nd ed., pp. 48–66). New York: Routledge.

Guinier, L., & Torres, G. (2002). *The Miner's Canary: Enlisting Race, Resisting Power, Transforming Democracy.* Cambridge, MA: Harvard University Press.

Gutiérrez-Jones, C.S. (2001). *Critical Race Narratives: A Study of Race, Rhetoric, and Injury.* New York: New York University Press.

Gwaltney, J.L. (1993). *Drylongso: A Self Portrait of Black America.* New York: New Press.

Hacker, A. (1995). *Two Nations: Black and White, Separate, Hostile, Unequal* (Expanded and updated ed.). New York: Ballantine Books.

Haney-Lopez, I. (2006). *White By Law: The Legal Construction of Race.* New York: New York University Press.

Hardiman, R., & Jackson, B. (2007). Conceptual Foundations for Social Justice Education. In M. Adams, L.A. Bell & P. Griffin (Eds.), *Teaching for Diversity and Social Justice* (2nd ed., pp. 35–48). New York: Routledge.

Harding, V. (1990). *Hope and History: Why We Must Share the Story of the Movement.* Maryknoll, NY: Orbis Books.

Harris, A., Carney, S., & Fine, M. (2001). Counter Work: Introduction to "Under the Covers: Theorizing the Politics of Counterstories." *The International Journal of Critical Psychology, 4,* 6–18.

Herring, C. (2006). Is Discrimination Dead? In M.H. Durr & A. Shirley (Eds.), *Race, Work and Family in the Lives of African Americans* (pp. 3–12). Lanham, MD: Rowman & Littlefield.

Hill Collins, P. (2000). *Black Feminist Thought: Knowledge, Consciousness, and the Politics of Empowerment* (2nd ed.). New York: Routledge.

Hitchcock, J. (2002). *Lifting the White Veil: An Exploration of White American Culture in a Multiracial Context.* Roselle, NJ: Crandall Dostie & Douglass Books.

Hochschild, J.L. (1995). *Facing Up to the American Dream: Race, Class, and the Soul of the Nation.* Princeton, NJ: Princeton University Press.

hooks, b. (1989). *Talking Back: Thinking Feminist, Thinking Black.* Boston, MA: South End Press.

hooks, b. (1990). *Feminist Theory: From Margin to Center.* Cambridge, MA: South End Press.

hooks, b. (1994). *Teaching to Transgress: Education as the Practice of Freedom.* New York: Routledge.

HoSang, D. (2006). Beyond Policy: Ideology, Race and the Reimagining of Youth. In S. Ginwright, P. Noguera & J. Cammarota (Eds.), *Beyond Resistance!: Youth Activism and Community Change* (pp. 3–19). New York: Routledge.

Howard, G.R. (2006). *We Can't Teach What We Don't Know: White Teachers, Multiracial Schools* (2nd ed.). New York: Teachers College Press.

Isaacs, J. (2007). *Economic Mobility of Black and White Families.* Philadelphia, PA: Pew Charitable Trusts.

Kailin, J. (1999). Preparing Urban Teachers for Schools and Communities: An Antiracist Perspective. *The High School Journal, 82*(2), 80–88.

Katznelson, I. (2005). *When Affirmative Action Was White: An Untold History of Racial Inequality in Twentieth-Century America.* New York: W.W. Norton.

Kelley, R.D.G. (1996). *Race Rebels: Culture, Politics, and the Black Working Class.* New York: The Free Press.

Kelley, R.D.G., & Lewis, E. (2000). *To Make Our World Anew: A History of African Americans.* Oxford; New York: Oxford University Press.

Kendall, F. (2006). *Understanding White Privilege: Creating Pathways to Authentic Relationships across Race.* New York: Routledge.

Kirschke, A.H. (2007). *Art in Crisis: W.E.B. Du Bois and the Struggle for African American Identity and Memory.* Bloomington, IN: Indiana University Press.

Kitwana, B. (2002). *The Hip Hop Generation: Young Blacks and the Crisis in African-American Culture.* New York: Basic Books.

Kivel, P. (1996). *Uprooting Racism: How White People Can Work for Racial Justice.* Gabriola Island, BC; Philadelphia, PA: New Society Publishers.

Kluegel, J.R., & Smith, E. (1986). *Beliefs about Inequality: Americans' Views of What Is and What Ought To Be.* New York: de Gruyter.

Kohl, H. (2004). The Politics of Children's Literature: What's Wrong with the Rosa Parks Myth? In D. Menkart, A.D. Murray & J.L. Roem (Eds.), *Putting the Movement Back Into Civil Rights Teaching.* Washington, DC: Teaching for Change.

Korza, P., Schaffer, B.B., & Assaf, A. (2005). *Civic Dialogue, Arts and Culture: Findings from Animating Democracy.* Washington, DC: Americans for the Arts.

Ladson-Billings, G. (2009a). Just What is Critical Race Theory and What's it Doing in a Nice Field Like Education? In E. Taylor, D. Gillborn & G. Ladson-Billings (Eds.), *Foundations of Critical Race Theory in Education* (pp. 17–36). New York: Routledge.

Ladson-Billings, G. (2009b). *The Dreamkeepers: Successful Teachers of African American Children.* San Francisco, CA: John Wiley & Sons.

Ladson-Billings, G.T., & Tate, W.F. (2006). Toward a Critical Race Theory of Education. In A.R. Dixson & C.K. Rousseau (Eds.), *Critical Race*

Theory in Education: All God's Children Got a Song (pp. 11–30). New York: Routledge.

Levins Morales, A. (1998). *Medicine Stories: History, Culture, and the Politics of Integrity*. Cambridge, MA: South End Press.

Lewin, K. (1952). *Field Theory in Social Science: Selected Theoretical Papers*. London: Tavistock.

Lewis, A. (2003). Some Are More Equal Than Others: Lessons on Whiteness from School. In A.W. Doane & E. Bonilla-Silva (Eds.), *White Out: The Continuing Significance of Racism* (pp. 3–21). New York: Routledge.

Lipman, P. (2003). Chicago School Policy: Regulating Black and Latino Youth in the Global City. *Race, Ethnicity and Education, 6*(4), 331–355.

Lippard, L.R. (1984). *Get the Message?: A Decade of Art for Social Change*. New York: E.P. Dutton.

Lippard, L.R. (1990). *Mixed Blessings: New Art in a Multicultural America*. New York: Pantheon Books.

Lipsitz, G. (2006). *The Possessive Investment in Whiteness: How White People Profit from Identity Politics* (Rev. and expanded ed.). Philadelphia, PA: Temple University Press.

Loewen, J.W. (2006). *Sundown Towns: A Hidden Dimension of American Racism*. New York: Touchstone.

Love, B.J., & Phillips, K.J. (2007). Ageism and Adultism Curriculum Design. In M. Adams, L.A. Bell & P. Griffin (Eds.), *Teaching for Diversity and Social Justice* (2nd ed., pp. 359–380). New York: Routledge.

McCrary, N.E. (2000). Investigating the Use of Narrative in Affective Learning on Issues of Social Justice. *Theory and Research in Social Education, 30*(2), 255–273.

McIntosh, P. (1990). White Privilege: Unpacking the Invisible Knapsack. *Independent School, 49*, 31–36.

McIntyre, A. (1997). *Making Meaning of Whiteness: Exploring Racial Identity with White Teachers*. Albany, NY: SUNY Press.

McKinney, K.D. (2005). *Being White: Stories of Race and Racism*. New York: Routledge.

Marable, M. (2002). *The Great Wells of Democracy: The Meaning of Race in American Life*. New York: Basic Civitas Books.

Marx, S. (2006). *Revealing the Invisible: Confronting Passive Racism in Teacher Education*. New York: Routledge.

Massey, D.S., & Denton, N.A. (1993). *American Apartheid: Segregation and the Making of the Underclass*. Cambridge, MA: Harvard University Press.

Matsuda, M.J. (1996). *Where is Your Body?: And Other Essays on Race, Gender, and the Law*. Boston, MA: Beacon Press.

Menkart, D., Murray, A.D., & View, J.L. (Eds.). (2004). *Putting the Movement Back into Civil Rights Teaching*. Washington, DC: Teaching for Change.

Michie, G. (1999). *Holler If You Hear Me: The Education of a Teacher and His Students*. New York: Teachers College Press.

Morrell, E., & Duncan-Andrade, J. (2008). *The Art of Critical Pedagogy: Possibilities for Moving from Theory to Practice in Urban Schools*. New York: Peter Lang.

Morrison, T. (1993). Nobel Lecture, December 7, 1993, Nobel Foundation, http://nobelprize.org/nobel_prizes/literature/laureates/1993/morrison-lecture.html (accessed July 1, 2009).

Murray, T. (2006). Collaborative Knowledge Building and Integral Theory: On Perspectives, Uncertainty and Mutual Regard. *Integral Review, 2,* 210–268.

Myers, K.A. (2005). *Racetalk: Racism Hiding in Plain Sight.* New York: Rowman & Littlefield.

NCES (National Center for Education Statistics). (2007). *Schools and Staffing in the U.S.* Washington, DC: US Department of Education, Office of Educational Research and Improvement.

Noguera, P. (2003). *City Schools and the American Dream: Reclaiming the Promise of Public Education.* New York: Teachers College Press.

Noguera, P. (2008). *The Trouble with Black Boys: And Other Reflections on Race, Equity, and the Future of Public Education.* San Francisco, CA: Jossey-Bass.

Obama, B. (2008). *A More Perfect Union.* Speech on race delivered at National Constitutional Center, Philadelphia, PA, March 18, 2008, http://www.nytimes.com/2008/03/18/us/politics/18text-obama.html (accessed March 19, 2008).

Oliver, M.L., & Shapiro, T.M. (1997). *Black Wealth/White Wealth: A New Perspective on Racial Inequality.* New York: Routledge.

Omi, M., & Winant, H. (1986). *Racial Formation in the United States: From the 1960s to the 1980s.* New York: Routledge.

Parker, L., & Lynn, M. (2009). What's Race Got to Do With It?: Critical Race Theory's Conflicts With and Connections to Qualitative Research Methodology and Epistemology. In E. Taylor, D. Gillborn & G. Ladson-Billings (Eds.), *Foundations of Critical Race Theory in Education* (pp. 148–160). New York: Routledge.

Parker, W.C. (2003a). *Teaching Democracy: Unity and Diversity in Public Life.* New York: Teachers College Press.

Parker, W.C. (Ed.). (2003b). *Educating the Democratic Mind.* New York: SUNY Press.

Paulson, A.M., & Marks, A. (2008, March 21). Obama Speech Opens Up Race Dialogue. *The Christian Science Monitor,* http://www.christiansciencemonitor.com/2008/0321/p01s02-uspo.html (accessed June 3, 2008).

PBS. (2007). *Art: 21—Art in the Twenty-First Century* (TV series). New York: PBS.

Peck, J. (1994). Talk about Racism: Framing a Popular Discourse on Oprah Winfrey. *Cultural Critique, 27,* 89–126.

Perry, T. (2003). Freedom for Literacy and Literacy for Freedom: The African-American Philosophy of Education. In T. Perry, C. Steele A., & Hiliard (Eds.), *Young, Gifted and Black: Promoting High Achievement Among African American Students* (pp. 11–51). Boston, MA: Beacon Press.

Perry, T., Steele, C., & Hiliard, A. (2003). *Young, Gifted and Black: Promoting High Achievement Among African American Students.* Boston, MA: Beacon Press.

Pietri, P. (1973). *Puerto Rican Obituary*. New York: Monthly Review Press.

Roberts, R.A. (2005). *Radical Movements: Katherine Dunham and Ronald K. Brown Teaching Toward Critical Consciousness*. City University of New York Graduate Center, New York.

Roberts, R.A., Bell, L.A., & Murphy, B. (2008). Flipping the Script: Analyzing Youth Talk about Race and Racism. *Anthropology and Education Quarterly, 39*(3), 334–354.

Romney, P. (2005). The Art of Dialogue. In P. Korza, B.S. Bacon & A. Assaf (Eds.), *Civic Dialogue, Arts and Culture: Findings from Animating Democracy* (pp. 57–79). Washington, DC: Americans for the Arts.

Roy, B. (1999). *Bitters in the Honey: Tales of Hope and Disappointment across Divides of Race and Time*. Fayetteville: University of Arkansas Press.

Ryan, W. (1976). *Blaming the Victim* (Rev. and updated ed.). New York: Vintage Books.

Sack, K. (2008, June 5). Research Finds Wide Disparities in Health Care by Race and Region. *The New York Times*, http://www.nytimes.com/2008/06/05/health/research/05disparities.html (accessed July 8, 2008).

Sarbin, T.R. (1986). The Narrative as a Root Metaphor for Psychology. In T.R. Sarbin (Ed.), *Narrative Psychology: The Storied Nature of Human Conduct* (pp. 3–21). New York: Praeger.

Sarris, G. (1990). Storytelling in the Classroom: Crossing Vexed Chasms. *College English, 52*(2), 169–184.

Schoem, D., & Hurtado, S. (Eds.). (2001). *Integroup Dialogue: Deliberative Democracy in School, College, Community and Workplace*. Ann Arbor: University of Michigan Press.

Schutzman, M., & Cohen-Cruz, J. (1994). *Playing Boal: Theatre, Therapy, Activism*. New York: Routledge.

Scott, J.C. (1990). *Domination and the Arts of Resistance: Hidden Transcripts*. New Haven, CT: Yale University Press.

Shipler, D.K. (1997). *A Country of Strangers: Blacks and Whites in America*. New York: Knopf.

Silko, L. (1986). *Ceremony*. New York: Penguin Books.

Sleeter, C.E. (2007). *Facing Accountability in Education: Democracy and Equity at Risk*. New York: Teachers College Press.

Sleeter, C.E. (2008). Equity, Democracy, and Neoliberal Assaults on Teacher Education. *Teaching and Teacher Education, 24*, 1947–1957.

Smith, C. (2007). The Reality of White Privilege. In C. Smith (Ed.), *The Cost of Privilege: Taking on the System of White Supremacy and Racism* (pp. 234–249). Fayetteville, NC: Camino Press.

Smitherman, G., & van Dijk, T.A. (1988). *Discourse and Discrimination*. Detroit, MI: Wayne State University Press.

Solarzano, D., & Yosso, T. (2002). Critical Race Methodology: Counter-Storytelling as an Analytic Framework for Education Research. *Qualitative Inquiry, 8*, 23–44.

Solorzano, D.G., Ceja, M., & Yosso, T. (2000). Critical Race Theory, Racial Microaggressions, and Campus Climate: The Experiences of African American Students. *Journal of Negro Education, 69*(1/2), 60–73.

Solorzano, D.G., & Delgado-Bernal, D. (2001). Examining Transformational Resistance through a Critical Race and Latcrit Theory Framework: Chicana and Chicano Students in an Urban Context. *Urban Education, 36*(3), 308–342.

Soohoo, S. (2006). *Talking Leaves: Narratives of Otherness.* Cresskill, NJ: Hampton Press.

Spring, J. (2004). *Deculturalization and the Struggle for Equality: A Brief History of Dominated Cultures in the United States.* Boston, MA: McGraw-Hill.

Stannard, D.E. (1992). *American Holocaust: Columbus and the Conquest of the New World.* New York: Oxford University Press.

Steinhorn, L., & Diggs-Brown, B. (1999). *By the Color of Our Skin: The Illusion of Integration and the Reality of Race.* New York: Dutton.

Symcox, L. (2002). *Whose History?: The Struggle for National Standards in American Classrooms.* New York: Teachers College Press.

Tatum, B.D. (1997). *"Why Are All the Black Kids Sitting Together in the Cafeteria?" and Other Conversations about Race.* New York: Basic Books.

Tatum, B.D. (2003). *Why Are All the Black Kids Sitting Together in the Cafeteria?* New York: Basic Books.

Thompson, A. (1997). For: Anti-Racist Education. *Curriculum Inquiry, 27*(1), 7–44.

Tuckman, B.W, & Jensen, M.A.C. (1977). Stages of Small Group Development Revisited. *Group and Organizational Studies, 2,* 419–427.

Valenzuela, A. (1999). *Subtractive Schooling: U.S. Mexican Youth and the Politics of Caring.* New York: SUNY Press.

van Dijk, T.A. (1984). *Prejudice in Discourse: An Analysis of Ethnic Prejudice in Cognition and Conversation.* Amsterdam: John Benjamins.

van Dijk, T.A. (1993). *Elite Discourse and Racism.* Newbury Park, CA: Sage Publications.

van Dijk, T.A. (1999). Discourse and the Denial of Racism. In A.N.C. Jaworski (Ed.), *The Discourse Reader* (pp. 541–558). London: Routledge.

Vickery, P. (2008). Progressive Pedagogy in the U.S. History Survey. *Radical Teacher, 83,* 10–13.

Villega, A.M., & Lucas, T. (2002). *Educating Culturally Responsive Teachers: A Coherent Approach.* New York: SUNY Press.

Wacquant, L.J.D. (2009). *Punishing the Poor: The Neoliberal Government of Social Insecurity* (English language ed.). Durham, NC: Duke University Press.

Walsh, K.C. (2007). *Talking about Race: Community Dialogues and the Politics of Difference.* Chicago, IL: University of Chicago Press.

Ward, J.V. (1996). Raising Resisters: The Role of Truth Telling in the Psychological Lives of African American Girls. In B. Leadbeater & N. Way (Eds.), *Urban Girls: Resisting Stereotypes, Creating Identities* (pp. 85–99). New York: New York University Press.

Ward, J.V. (2000). *The Skin We're In: Teaching Black Children to be Emotionally Strong, Socially Smart, Spiritually Connected.* New York: Free Press.

Wetherell, M., & Potter, J. (1992). *Mapping the Language of Racism: Discourse and the Legitimation of Exploitation.* New York: Columbia University Press.

Williams, P.J. (1991). *The Alchemy of Race and Rights.* Cambridge, MA: Harvard University Press.

Williams, P.J. (1998). *Seeing a Color-Blind Future: The Paradox of Race.* New York: Noonday Press.

Willis, P.E. (1981). *Learning to Labor: How Working Class Kids Get Working Class Jobs.* New York: Columbia University Press.

Wilson, D. (2005). *Inventing Black-on-Black Violence: Discourse, Space, and Representation.* Syracuse, NY: Syracuse University Press.

Winant, H. (2004). *The New Politics of Race: Globalism, Difference, Justice.* Minneapolis: University of Minnesota Press.

Wise, T.J. (2005). *White Like Me.* Brooklyn, NY; Berkeley, CA: Soft Skull Press.

Wise, T.J. (2005). *Affirmative Action: Racial Preference in Black and White.* New York: Routledge.

Wortham, S. (2000). Interactional Positioning and Narrative Construction. *Narrative Inquiry, 10*(1), 157–184.

Wright, R. (2005). *Stolen Continents: Five Hundred Years of Conquest and Resistance in the Americas.* Boston, MA: Houghton Mifflin.

Yeskel, F., & Wright, B. (2007). Classism Curriculum Design. In M. Adams, L.A. Bell & P. Griffin (Eds.), *Teaching for Diversity and Social Justice* (2nd ed., pp. 232–260). New York: Routledge.

Yosso, T. (2006). *Critical Race Counterstories along the Chicana/Chicano Educational Pipeline.* New York: Routledge.

Zinn, H. (2003). *A People's History of the United States: 1942–present* (New ed.). New York: HarperCollins.

Zuniga, X., Nagda, B.A., Chesler, M., & Cytron-Walker, A. (2007). *Intergroup Dialogues in Higher Education: Meaningful Learning about Social Justice.* San Francisco, CA: Jossey-Bass.

Zuniga, X., Nagda, B.A., & Sevig, T.D. (2002). Intergroup Dialogues: An Educational Model for Cultivating Engagement across Differences. *Equity and Excellence in Education, 35*(1), 7–17.

Index

Page numbers in italics refer to figures.

W
Wagner Act of 1935, 54
wealth, 54–55
white: advantage, 57, 102–103;
dominance, 33–34; privilege, 14, 29,
54–55; students, 81, 84; supremacy,
14; talk, 33–34
white people: beliefs of, 30–31; and
concealed stories, 45–46; discomfort
of, 103; and race talk, 2, 33–34; racial
position of, 82; socialization of, 50;
and wealth, 54–55

whitestream, 18–19
Williams, Patricia, 81
Wilson, Fred, 52
Wright, Jeremiah, 45

Y
Yosso, Tara, 23
young people. *See* youth
youth: poetry of, 101; and resilience,
65–66; resistance by, 63–69; and
resistance stories, 67–69; stereotypes
about, 63